JEWISH COOKING

JEWISH COOKING

130 CLASSIC DISHES SHOWN IN 220 EVOCATIVE PHOTOGRAPHS

MARLENA SPIELER

southwater

This edition is published by Southwater,
an imprint of Anness Publishing Ltd,
Blaby Road, Wigston, Leicestershire LE18 4SE;
info@anness.com

www.southwaterbooks.com;
www.annesspublishing.com

If you like the images in this book and would like to
investigate using them for publishing, promotions
or advertising, please visit our website
www.practicalpictures.com for more information.

A CIP catalogue record for this book is available
from the British Library.

Publisher: Joanna Lorenz
Editor: Amy Christian
Photography: William Lingwood
Production Controller: Wendy Lawson

Designed and edited for Anness Publishing Ltd by
the Bridgewater Book Company Ltd

Publisher's Acknowledgments
All photographs are by William Lingwood except
the following: p188 AKG; p189 The Bridgeman Art
Library; pp 190, 191 Hulton Getty Images.

Front cover shows Chamin – for recipe, see page 19.

PUBLISHER'S NOTE
Although the advice and information in this book
are believed to be accurate and true at the time of
going to press, neither the authors nor the publisher
can accept any legal responsibility or liability for any
errors or omissions that may have been made nor
for any inaccuracies nor for any loss, harm or injury
that comes about from following instructions or
advice in this book.

NOTES
For all recipes, quantities are given in both
metric and imperial measures and, where
appropriate, in standard cups and spoons.
Follow one set of measures, but not a
mixture, because they are not
interchangeable.
  Standard spoon and cup measures are
level. 1 tsp = 5ml, 1 tbsp = 15ml, 1 cup =
250ml/8fl oz.
Australian standard tablespoons are 20ml.
Australian readers should use 3 tsp in place
of 1 tbsp for measuring small quantities.
American pints are 16fl oz/2 cups. American
readers should use 20fl oz/2.5 cups in place
of 1 pint when measuring liquids.
  Electric oven temperatures in this book are
for conventional ovens. When using a fan
oven, the temperature will probably need to
be reduced by about 10–20°C/20–40°F.
Since ovens vary, you should check with your
manufacturer's instruction book for guidance.
  The nutritional analysis given for each
recipe is calculated per portion (i.e. serving
or item), unless otherwise stated. If the recipe
gives a range, such as Serves 4–6, then the
nutritional analysis will be for the smaller
portion size, i.e. 6 servings. The analysis does
not include optional ingredients, such as salt
added to taste.
  Medium (US large) eggs are used unless
otherwise stated.

Contents

Introduction

Jewish food: the phrase conjures up images of borscht, chicken soup with matzo balls, salt beef and chopped liver. These certainly are Jewish foods, relished by generations of Eastern European Jews, but Jewish cuisine is much, much more varied than that.

I grew up in California. The foods we ate were those of West Coast America – artichokes and oranges and avocados – but our culinary souls were also nourished by the foods of the Old Country of our grandparents' era: *kasha*, *gedempte flaiche* and *knaidlach*, *matzo brei* and *kishke* from Ashkenazi Russia, Poland, the Ukraine and Lithuania, all served with a delicious overlay of Old New York.

Jewish food is a combination of richly varied cuisines from all over the globe, reflecting the multi-ethnicity of the Jewish people, and the many places where they have settled over the course of time. For years I thought the little savoury pastries called *empanadas* were typically Jewish, because that's what my cousin used to make when we visited her. It was only years later that I discovered they were native to Uruguay, where she was raised.

In the past, the Ashkenazim and Sephardim were often far removed from each other; the spicy food of the Sephardim was seldom served on traditional Ashkenazi tables and vice versa. The establishment of the State of Israel, migration and the expansion of modern travel have changed this considerably, and brought Jews together again, starting at the table where they can share their own flavours and dishes.

Regardless of where history has taken them, the food Jews eat is governed by the laws of Kashrut – the code of fitness that applies to what may be eaten, how food must be prepared and which foods can be combined with other foods. There are variations in how different ethnic groups adhere to Kashrut, and degrees of observance, but the basics are the same. Certain types of meat, fish and

BELOW: *Kofta kebabs are very popular in Jewish communities from the Middle East.*

ABOVE: *Fragrant beetroot (beet) and vegetable soup with spiced lamb kubbeh.*

ABOVE: *Filo-wrapped fish – best served with a zesty tomato sauce.*

ABOVE: *Fried matzo meal and cottage cheese latkes.*

fowl are allowed, while others are forbidden. Rules govern the slaughter and inspection of animals, as well as which parts may be used, and there is an injunction against combining meat foods with dairy foods. This set of rules has kept the Jewish people culturally distinct, as well as giving an underlying flavour to their food.

The preparation, eating and rituals involved with Kashrut have always played an important part in the lives of the Jewish people. In the Torah, the Patriarch Abraham is noted for the hospitable table he sets. It is recorded that Isaac asked his son for a nice dish of savoury meat, and also that Esau sold his birthright for a big,

soupy lentil stew. In Chapter 11 of the book of Numbers, the story is told of how the Israelites fleeing Egypt wept with longing for the garlic and leeks they had eaten during their captivity – even freedom lacked flavour without delicious seasonings.

The noted Andalucian-Egyptian philosopher and physician Moses Maimonides (Moses ben Maimon) emphasized the importance of serenity of spirit, both for cook and diner. He also stressed the value of eating healthy food, prepared appealingly. Sharing sociable meals, he suggested, not only made for a happier, less anxious individual; it also bridged the differences between ethnic groups.

When Jews gather together, we eat, and what we eat are often the traditional foods, because each food has its own story. The flavour of remembrance seasons all our meals as we recall where we have wandered and who we met along the way, the meals we shared and the ingredients that filled our pots along each mile, in every place.

In this book I would like to share with you my favourite recipes from various Jewish communities throughout the world, and from my own life and traditions as well. In the words of the Hebrew expression that translates as *bon appetit*, I wish you all *B'tay avon*.   **Marlena Spieler**

Soups, appetizers and brunch

From chopped liver to aubergine

(eggplant) salads, Jewish appetizers are

adored by everyone. Festive meals from

the weekly Shabbat to annual holidays

almost always include a selection of

appetizers and what often distinguishes an

everyday meal from a celebration is the

serving of these delicacies.

Tomato soup with Israeli couscous

Israeli couscous is a toasted, round pasta, which is much larger than regular couscous. It makes a wonderful addition to this warm and comforting soup. If you like your soup really garlicky, add an extra clove of chopped garlic just before serving.

SERVES 4–6

30ml/2 tbsp olive oil

1 onion, chopped

1–2 carrots, diced

400g/14oz can chopped tomatoes

6 garlic cloves, roughly chopped

1.5 litres/2^1/$_2$ pints/6^1/$_4$ cups vegetable or chicken stock

200–250g/7–9oz/1–1^1/$_2$ cups Israeli couscous

2–3 mint sprigs, chopped, or several pinches of dried mint

1.5ml/^{1}/$_4$ tsp ground cumin

^{1}/$_4$ bunch fresh coriander (cilantro), or about 5 sprigs, chopped

cayenne pepper, to taste

salt and ground black pepper

1 Heat the oil in a large pan, then add the onion and carrots and cook gently for about 10 minutes until softened.

2 Add the tomatoes, half the garlic, stock, couscous, mint, ground cumin, coriander, and cayenne pepper, salt and pepper to taste.

3 Bring the soup to the boil, add the remaining chopped garlic, then reduce the heat slightly and simmer gently for 7–10 minutes, stirring occasionally, or until the couscous is just tender.

4 Serve piping hot, ladled into individual serving bowls.

Nutritional information per portion: Energy 130kcal/541kJ; Protein 2.6g; Carbohydrate 21.3g, of which sugars 3.9g; Fat 4.3g, of which saturates 0.6g; Cholesterol 0mg; Calcium 19mg; Fibre 1.3g; Sodium 11mg.

Lubiya

This delicious Sephardi Israeli soup, of black-eyed beans and turmeric-tinted tomato broth, is flavoured with tangy lemon and speckled with chopped fresh coriander. It is ideal for serving at parties – simply multiply the quantities as required.

SERVES 4

175g/6oz/1 cup black-eyed beans (peas)
15ml/1 tbsp olive oil
2 onions, chopped
4 garlic cloves, chopped
1 medium-hot fresh chilli, chopped
5ml/1 tsp ground cumin
5ml/1 tsp ground turmeric
250g/9oz fresh or canned
**   tomatoes, diced**
600ml/1 pint/2¹/₂ cups chicken,
**   beef or vegetable stock**
25g/1oz fresh coriander (cilantro) leaves,
**   roughly chopped**
juice of ¹/₂ lemon
pitta bread, to serve

1 Put the beans in a pan, cover with cold water, bring to the boil, then cook for 5 minutes. Remove from the heat, cover and leave to stand for 2 hours.

2 Drain the beans, return to the pan, cover with fresh cold water, then simmer for 35–40 minutes, or until the beans are tender. Drain and set aside.

3 Heat the oil in a pan, add the onions, garlic and chilli and cook for 5 minutes, or until the onion is soft.

4 Stir in the cumin, turmeric, tomatoes, stock, half the coriander and the beans and simmer for 20 minutes. Stir in the lemon juice and remaining coriander and serve at once with pitta bread.

Nutritional information per portion: Energy 172kcal/727kJ; Protein 10.9g; Carbohydrate 25.4g, of which sugars 6g; Fat 3.7g, of which saturates 0.6g; Cholesterol 0mg; Calcium 73mg; Fibre 8.5g; Sodium 17mg.

Chicken soup with knaidlach

A bowl of chicken soup can heal the soul as well as the body, as anyone who has ever suffered from flu and been comforted, or suffered grief and been consoled, will know. This is why this warming soup is often known as the Jewish antibiotic.

SERVES 6–8

1–1.5kg/2¼–3¼lb chicken, cut
    into portions
2–3 onions, kept whole
3–4 litres/5–7 pints/12–16 cups water
3–5 carrots, thickly sliced
3–5 celery sticks, thickly sliced
1 small parsnip, cut in half
30–45ml/2–3 tbsp chopped fresh parsley
30–45ml/2–3 tbsp chopped fresh dill
1–2 pinches ground turmeric
2 chicken stock (bouillon) cubes, crumbled
2 garlic cloves, finely chopped (optional)
salt and ground black pepper

FOR THE KNAIDLACH

175g/6oz/¾ cup medium matzo meal
2 eggs, lightly beaten
45ml/3 tbsp vegetable oil or rendered
    chicken fat
1 garlic clove, finely chopped (optional)
30ml/2 tbsp chopped fresh parsley, plus
    extra to garnish
½ onion, finely grated
1–2 pinches of chicken stock (bouillon)
    cube or powder (optional)
about 90ml/6 tbsp water

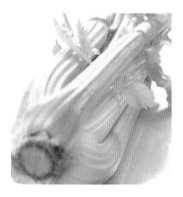

1 Put the chicken pieces in a large pan. Keeping them whole, cut a large cross in the stem end of each onion and add to the pan with the water, carrots, celery, parsnip, parsley, half the dill, the turmeric, and salt and black pepper.

2 Cover the pan and bring to the boil, then immediately lower the heat to a simmer. Skim and discard the scum that surfaces to the top. (Scum will continue to form but it is only the first scum that rises that will detract from the clarity and flavour of the soup.)

3 Add the crumbled stock cubes and simmer for 2–3 hours. When the soup is flavourful, skim off the fat. Alternatively, chill the soup and remove the layer of solid fat that forms.

4 To make the knaidlach, in a large bowl combine the matzo meal with the eggs, oil or fat, chopped garlic, if using, parsley, onion, salt and pepper. Add only a little chicken stock cube or powder, if using, as these are salty. Add the water and mix together until the mixture is the consistency of a thick, soft paste.

5 Cover the matzo batter and chill for 30 minutes, during which time the mixture will become firm.

6 Bring a pan of water to the boil and have a bowl of water next to the stove. Dip two tablespoons into the water, then take a spoonful of the matzo batter. With wet hands, roll it into a ball, then slip it into the boiling water and reduce the heat so that the water simmers. Continue with the remaining matzo batter, working quickly, then cover the pan and cook for 15 minutes.

7 Remove the knaidlach from the pan with a slotted spoon and transfer to a plate for about 20 minutes to firm up.

8 To serve, reheat the soup, adding the remaining dill and the garlic, if using. Put two to three knaidlach in each bowl, pour over the hot soup and garnish.

Nutritional information per portion: Energy 266kcal/1115kJ; Protein 25.7g; Carbohydrate 24g, of which sugars 6.6g; Fat 7.5g, of which saturates 1.2g; Cholesterol 109mg; Calcium 48mg; Fibre 2.7g; Sodium 86mg.

Hungarian cherry soup

Soups made from seasonal fruits are a favourite Central European treat, and cherry soup is one of the glories of the Hungarian table. It is often served at the start of a dairy meal, such as at the festival of Shavuot when dairy foods are traditionally feasted upon.

SERVES 6

1kg/2¼lb fresh, frozen or canned
    sour cherries, such as Morello
    or Montmorency, pitted
250ml/8fl oz/1 cup water
175–250g/6–9oz/about 1 cup sugar,
    to taste
1–2 cinnamon sticks, each about
    5cm/2in long
750ml/1¼ pints/3 cups dry red wine
5ml/1 tsp almond extract, or to taste
250ml/8fl oz/1 cup single (light) cream
250ml/8fl oz/1 cup sour cream or
    crème fraîche

1 Put the pitted cherries, water, sugar, cinnamon and wine in a large pan. Bring to the boil, lower the heat and leave to simmer for about 20–30 minutes until the cherries are tender. Remove from the heat and add the almond extract.

2 In a bowl, stir a few tablespoons of single cream into the sour cream or crème fraîche to thin it down, then stir in the rest until the mixture is smooth. Stir the mixture into the cherry soup, then leave to chill until ready to serve.

Nutritional information per portion: Energy 484kcal/2037kJ; Protein 3.7g; Carbohydrate 64.1g, of which sugars 64.1g; Fat 16.3g, of which saturates 10.3g; Cholesterol 48mg; Calcium 125mg; Fibre 1g; Sodium 53mg.

Sweet and sour cabbage, beetroot and tomato borscht

There are many delicious variations of this classic Ashkenazi soup, which may be served either hot or cold with slices of buttered rye bread. This version includes plentiful amounts of cabbage, tomatoes and potatoes to make it into a substantial meal.

SERVES 6

1 onion, chopped

1 carrot, chopped

4–6 raw or cooked, not pickled beetroot (beets), 3–4 diced and 1–2 grated

400g/14oz can tomatoes

4–6 new potatoes, cut into bitesize pieces

1 small white cabbage, thinly sliced

1 litre/1¾ pints/4 cups vegetable stock

45ml/3 tbsp sugar

30–45ml/2–3 tbsp white wine vinegar

45ml/3 tbsp chopped fresh dill, plus extra to garnish

salt and ground black pepper

sour cream, to garnish

buttered rye bread, to serve

1 Put the onion, carrot, diced beetroot, tomatoes, potatoes, cabbage and stock in a large pan. Bring to the boil, lower the heat and simmer for 30 minutes.

2 Add the grated beetroot, sugar and wine vinegar and cook for 10 minutes. Taste and add more sugar and/or vinegar if necessary. Season.

3 Stir the chopped dill into the soup and ladle into warmed soup bowls immediately.

4 Place a generous spoonful of sour cream in each bowl and sprinkle some extra chopped dill over the top. Serve the soup immediately with slices of buttered rye bread.

Nutritional information per portion: Energy 70kcal/294kJ; Protein 2.4g; Carbohydrate 14.7g, of which sugars 9.6g; Fat 0.6g, of which saturates 0.2g; Cholesterol 0mg; Calcium 32mg; Fibre 2.8g; Sodium 43mg.

Fragrant beetroot and vegetable soup with spiced lamb kubbeh

This tangy soup from the Jewish community of Cochin in India is served with dumplings made of bright yellow pasta wrapped around a spicy lamb filling and a dollop of green herb paste.

SERVES 6–8

15ml/1 tbsp vegetable oil
1/2 onion, finely chopped
6 garlic cloves
1 carrot, diced
1 courgette (zucchini), diced
1/2 celery stick, diced (optional)
4–5 cardamom pods
2.5ml/1/2 tsp curry powder
4 cooked, not pickled, beetroot (beets),
    finely diced and juice reserved
1 litre/1³/4 pints/4 cups
    vegetable stock
400g/14oz can chopped tomatoes
45–60ml/3–4 tbsp chopped fresh
    coriander (cilantro) leaves
2 bay leaves
15ml/1 tbsp sugar
salt and ground black pepper
15–30ml/1–2 tbsp white wine vinegar,
    to serve

FOR THE KUBBEH

2 large pinches of saffron threads
15ml/1 tbsp hot water
15ml/1 tbsp vegetable oil
1 large onion, chopped
250g/9oz lean minced (ground) lamb
5ml/1 tsp vinegar
1/2 bunch fresh mint, chopped
115g/4oz/1 cup plain (all-purpose) flour
2–3 pinches of salt
2.5–5ml/1/2–1 tsp ground turmeric
45–60ml/3–4 tbsp cold water

FOR THE GREEN HERB PASTE

4 garlic cloves, chopped
15–25ml/1–11/2 tbsp chopped
    fresh root ginger
1/2–4 fresh mild chillies
1/2 large bunch fresh coriander (cilantro)
30ml/2 tbsp white wine vinegar
extra virgin olive oil

1 For the paste, process the garlic, ginger and chillies in a food processor. Add the coriander, vinegar, oil and salt and process to a purée. Set aside.

2 For the kubbeh filling, leave the saffron and hot water to infuse (steep). Heat the oil in a pan and fry the onion until softened. Blend the onion and saffron water in a food processor. Add the lamb, season and blend. Add the vinegar and mint, then chill.

3 For the kubbeh dough, put the flour, salt and turmeric in a food processor, then gradually add the water, processing until it forms a sticky dough. Knead on a floured surface for 5 minutes, wrap in a plastic bag and leave for 30 minutes.

4 Divide the dough into 10–15 pieces. Roll each into a ball, then, using a pasta machine, roll into very thin rounds. Lay the rounds on a floured surface. Place a spoonful of filling in the middle of each. Dampen the edges of the dough, then seal. Set aside on a floured surface.

5 To make the soup, heat the oil in a pan and fry the onion for 10 minutes, or until softened. Add half the garlic, the carrot, courgette, celery, if using, cardamom and curry powder, and cook for 2–3 minutes. Add three of the diced beetroot, the stock, tomatoes, coriander, bay leaves and sugar to the pan. Bring to the boil, then lower the heat and simmer for about 20 minutes. Add the remaining beetroot, beetroot juice and garlic. Season and set aside until ready to serve.

6 To serve, reheat the soup and poach the dumplings in a large pan of salted boiling water for about 4 minutes. Using a slotted spoon, transfer the dumplings to a plate as they are cooked.

7 Ladle the soup into bowls, adding a dash of vinegar to each bowl, then add two or three dumplings and a small spoonful of the ginger and coriander paste to each. Serve immediately.

Nutritional information per portion: Energy 175kcal/732kJ; Protein 9.2g; Carbohydrate 18.6g, of which sugars 6.6g; Fat 7.6g, of which saturates 2.4g; Cholesterol 24mg; Calcium 69mg; Fibre 2.8g; Sodium 50mg.

Chamim

This Sephardi Shabbat dish of savoury meats and beans is baked in a very low oven for several hours. A parcel of rice is often added to the broth part way through cooking, which produces a lightly pressed rice with a slightly chewy texture.

SERVES 8

45ml/3 tbsp olive oil
1 onion, chopped
10 garlic cloves, chopped
1 parsnip, sliced
3 carrots, sliced
5–10ml/1–2 tsp ground cumin
2.5ml/¹/₂ tsp ground turmeric
15ml/1 tbsp chopped fresh root ginger
250g/9oz/1 cup chickpeas,
    soaked overnight and drained
2 litres/3¹/₂ pints/8 cups beef stock
1 potato, peeled and cut into chunks
¹/₂ marrow (large zucchini), sliced

400g/14oz fresh or canned
    tomatoes, diced
45–60ml/3–4 tbsp brown or green lentils
2 bay leaves
250g/9oz salted meat such as
    salt beef (or double the quantity
    of lamb)
250g/9oz piece of lamb
¹/₂ large bunch fresh coriander (cilantro),
    chopped
200g/7oz/1 cup long grain rice
1 lemon, cut into wedges, and a spicy
    sauce such as zchug or fresh chillies,
    finely chopped, to serve

1 Preheat the oven to 120°C/250°F/Gas ¹/₂. Heat the oil in a flameproof casserole, add the onion, garlic, parsnip, carrots and spices and cook for 2–3 minutes. Add the chickpeas, stock, potato, marrow, tomatoes, lentils, bay leaves, meat and coriander. Cover and cook in the oven for 3 hours.

2 Put the rice on a double thickness of muslin (cheesecloth) and tie together loosely at the corners.

3 Two hours before the end of cooking, place the parcel in the casserole, anchoring the edge of it under the lid so the parcel is allowed to steam. Cook for a further 2 hours.

4 Remove the rice. Skim any fat off the top of the soup and ladle it into bowls, adding some rice and pieces of meat to each. Serve with lemon wedges and spicy sauce or chillies.

Nutritional information per portion: Energy 463kcal/1941kJ; Protein 28.5g; Carbohydrate 60.5g, of which sugars 17g; Fat 12.7g, of which saturates 3.5g; Cholesterol 47mg; Calcium 130mg; Fibre 9.4g; Sodium 409mg.

Old country mushroom, bean and barley soup

This hearty Ashkenazi soup is perfect on a freezing cold day. Serve the soup in warmed bowls, with plenty of rye or pumpernickel bread.

SERVES 6–8

30–45ml/2–3 tbsp small haricot (navy)
   beans, soaked overnight
45–60ml/ 3–4 tbsp green split peas
45–60ml/3–4 tbsp yellow split peas
90–105ml/6–7 tbsp pearl barley
1 onion, chopped
2 carrots, sliced
3 celery sticks, diced or sliced
1/2 baking potato, peeled and cut
   into chunks
10g/1/4oz or 45ml/3 tbsp mixed
   flavourful dried mushrooms
5 garlic cloves, sliced
2 litres/31/2 pints/8 cups water
2 vegetable stock (bouillon) cubes
salt and ground black pepper
30–45ml/2–3 tbsp chopped fresh parsley,
   to garnish

1 In a large pan, put the beans, green and yellow split peas, pearl barley, onion, carrots, celery, potato, mushrooms, garlic and water.

2 Bring the mixture to the boil, then lower the heat, cover and simmer gently for about 1 1/2 hours, or until the beans are tender.

3 Crumble the stock cubes into the soup and taste for seasoning. Ladle into warmed bowls, garnish with chopped parsley and serve with rye or pumpernickel bread.

Nutritional information per portion: Energy 162kcal/689kJ; Protein 6.8g; Carbohydrate 34.1g, of which sugars 4.3g; Fat 0.8g, of which saturates 0.1g; Cholesterol 0mg; Calcium 34mg; Fibre 2.9g; Sodium 30mg.

Russian spinach and root vegetable soup with dill

This is a typical Russian soup, traditionally prepared when the first vegetables of springtime appear. Earthy root vegetables are enlivened with a tart topping of dill, lemon and sour cream.

SERVES 4–6

1 small turnip, cut into chunks
2 carrots, sliced or diced
1 small parsnip, cut into large dice
1 potato, peeled and diced
1 onion, chopped or cut into chunks
1 garlic clove, finely chopped
¼ celeriac bulb, diced
1 litre/1¾ pints/4 cups vegetable stock
200g/7oz spinach, roughly chopped
1 small bunch fresh dill, chopped
salt and ground black pepper

FOR THE GARNISH

2 hard-boiled eggs, sliced
1 lemon, sliced
250ml/8fl oz/1 cup sour cream
30ml/2 tbsp chopped fresh parsley
**   and dill**

1 Put the turnip, carrots, parsnip, potato, onion, garlic, celeriac and stock into a large pan. Bring to the boil, then simmer for 25–30 minutes, or until the vegetables are very tender.

2 Add the spinach to the pan and cook for a further 5 minutes, or until the spinach is tender but still green and leafy. Season with salt and pepper.

3 Stir the dill into the soup, then ladle into bowls and serve garnished with egg, lemon, sour cream and a sprinkling of parsley and dill.

Nutritional information per portion: Energy 49kcal/207kJ; Protein 2.1g; Carbohydrate 9.4g, of which sugars 5.1g; Fat 0.7g, of which saturates 0.1g; Cholesterol 0mg; Calcium 83mg; Fibre 2.8g; Sodium 58mg.

A potage of lentils

This soup is sometimes known as Esau's soup and may be served as part of a meal for Shabbat or as a meze the next day. Red lentils and vegetables are cooked and puréed, then sharpened with lots of lemon juice.

SERVES 4

45ml/3 tbsp olive oil
1 onion, chopped
2 celery sticks, chopped
1–2 carrots, sliced
8 garlic cloves, chopped
1 potato, peeled and diced
250g/9oz/generous 1 cup red lentils
1 litre/1³/₄ pints/4 cups
   vegetable stock
2 bay leaves

1–2 lemons, halved
2.5ml/¹/₂ tsp ground cumin, or
   to taste
cayenne pepper or Tabasco sauce,
   to taste
salt and ground black pepper
lemon slices and chopped
   fresh flat leaf parsley leaves,
   to serve

1 Heat the oil in a large pan. Add the onion and cook for about 5 minutes, or until softened. Stir in the celery, carrots, half the garlic and all the potato. Cook for a few minutes until beginning to soften.

2 Add the lentils and stock to the pan and bring to the boil. Lower the heat, cover and simmer for about 30 minutes, or until the potato and lentils are tender.

3 Add the bay leaves, remaining garlic and half the lemons to the pan and cook the soup for a further 10 minutes. Remove the bay leaves. Squeeze the juice from the remaining lemons, then stir into the soup, to taste.

4 Pour the soup into a food processor or blender and process until smooth. (You may need to do this in batches.) Pour the soup back into the pan, stir in the cumin, cayenne pepper or Tabasco sauce, and season with salt and pepper to taste.

5 Ladle the soup into bowls and top each portion with lemon slices and a sprinkling of chopped fresh flat leaf parsley.

Nutritional information per portion: Energy 308kcal/1297kJ; Protein 14.8g; Carbohydrate 44g, of which sugars 4.9g; Fat 9.3g, of which saturates 1.4g; Cholesterol 0mg; Calcium 48mg; Fibre 4.3g; Sodium 42mg.

Hummus

This classic Middle Eastern dish is made from cooked chickpeas, ground to a paste and flavoured with garlic, lemon juice, tahini, olive oil and cumin. It is delicious served with wedges of toasted pitta bread or crudités.

SERVES 4–6

400g/14oz can chickpeas, drained
60ml/4 tbsp tahini
2–3 garlic cloves, chopped
juice of 1/2–1 lemon

cayenne pepper
small pinch to 1.5ml/1/4 tsp ground
   cumin, or more to taste
salt and ground black pepper

1 Using a potato masher or food processor, coarsely mash the chickpeas. If you prefer a smoother purée, process them in a food processor or blender until smooth.

2 Mix the tahini into the chickpeas, then stir in the garlic, lemon juice, cayenne, cumin and salt and pepper to taste. If needed, add a little water. Serve at room temperature.

Nutritional information per portion: Energy 140kcal/586kJ; Protein 6.9g; Carbohydrate 11.2g, of which sugars 0.4g; Fat 7.8g, of which saturates 1.1g; Cholesterol 0mg; Calcium 97mg; Fibre 3.6g; Sodium 149mg.

Baba ghanoush

The quantities in this richly flavoured Middle Eastern aubergine dip can be varied according to taste. Adjust the amount of aubergine, garlic and lemon juice depending on how creamy, garlicky or tart you want the dip to be.

SERVES 2–4

1 large or 2 medium
    aubergines (eggplants)
2–4 garlic cloves, chopped, to taste
90–150ml/6–10 tbsp tahini
juice of 1 lemon, or to taste
1.5ml/¼ tsp ground cumin, or
    to taste
salt
extra virgin olive oil, for drizzling
coriander (cilantro) leaves, hot pepper
    sauce and a few olives and/or
    pickled cucumbers and (bell)
    peppers, to garnish
pitta bread or chunks of crusty French
    bread, to serve

1 Place the aubergine(s) directly over the flame of a gas stove or on the coals of a barbecue. Turn fairly frequently until deflated and the skin is evenly charred. Remove from the heat with a pair of tongs.

2 Put the aubergine(s) in a plastic bag or in a bowl and seal tightly. Leave to cool for 30–60 minutes.

3 Peel off the blackened skin from the aubergine(s), reserving the juices. Chop the flesh, either by hand for a textured result or in a food processor for a smooth purée. Put in a bowl and stir in the reserved juices.

4 Add the garlic and tahini to the aubergine and stir until smooth and well combined.

5 Stir in the lemon juice, which will thicken the mixture. If the mixture becomes too thick, add 15–30ml/ 1–2 tbsp water or more lemon juice. Season with cumin and salt to taste.

6 Spoon the mixture into a serving bowl. Drizzle with olive oil and garnish with coriander leaves, hot pepper sauce and olives and/or pickled cucumbers and peppers. Serve at room temperature with pitta bread or crusty French bread.

Nutritional information per portion: Energy 91kcal/375kJ; Protein 1g; Carbohydrate 2.2g, of which sugars 1.5g; Fat 8.8g, of which saturates 1.4g; Cholesterol 8mg; Calcium 8mg; Fibre 1.4g; Sodium 52mg.

Muhammara

This thick, roasted red pepper and walnut purée is beloved on the Sephardi table, especially in Syria. Serve it as a dip with spears of cos or romaine lettuce, wedges of pitta bread, chunks of tomato and slices of mozzarella cheese.

SERVES 4

1¹/₂ slices Granary (whole-wheat) bread, day-old or toasted

3 red (bell) peppers, roasted, skinned and chopped

2 very mild chillies, roasted, skinned and chopped

115g/4oz/1 cup walnut pieces

3–4 garlic cloves, chopped

15–30ml/1–2 tbsp balsamic vinegar or pomegranate molasses

juice of ¹/₂ lemon

2.5–5ml/¹/₂–1 tsp ground cumin

2.5ml/¹/₂ tsp sugar, or to taste

105ml/7 tbsp extra virgin olive oil

salt

1 Break the Granary bread into small pieces and place in a food processor or blender with all the remaining ingredients except the extra virgin olive oil. Blend together until all the ingredients are finely chopped.

2 With the motor running, slowly drizzle the extra virgin olive oil into the food processor or blender and process until the mixture forms a smooth paste. Spoon the muhammara into a serving dish and serve at room temperature.

Nutritional information per portion: Energy 444kcal/1833kJ; Protein 6.8g; Carbohydrate 15.5g, of which sugars 9.9g; Fat 39.8g, of which saturates 4.6g; Cholesterol 0mg; Calcium 62mg; Fibre 3.7g; Sodium 69mg.

Sun-dried tomato and pepper salad

This appetizer is very new-wave Tel Aviv – modern Mediterranean food that bridges the gap between Middle Eastern and contemporary European styles. It is good served with slices of very fresh bread or wedges of flat bread.

SERVES 4–6

10–15 sun-dried tomatoes

60–75ml/4–5 tbsp olive oil

3 yellow (bell) peppers, cut into bitesize pieces

6 garlic cloves, chopped

400g/14oz can chopped tomatoes

5ml/1 tsp fresh thyme leaves, or to taste

large pinch of sugar

15ml/1 tbsp balsamic vinegar

2–3 capers, rinsed and drained

15ml/1 tbsp chopped fresh parsley, or to taste

salt and ground black pepper

fresh thyme, to garnish (optional)

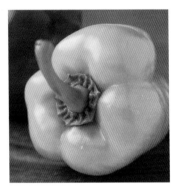

1 Put the sun-dried tomatoes in a bowl and pour over boiling water to cover. Leave to stand for at least 30 minutes until plumped up and juicy, then drain and cut the tomatoes into halves or quarters.

2 Heat the olive oil in a pan, add the peppers and cook for 5–7 minutes until lightly browned but not too soft.

3 Add half the garlic, the canned tomatoes, thyme and sugar and cook over a high heat, stirring occasionally, until the mixture is reduced to a thick paste. Season with salt and pepper to taste. Stir in the sun-dried tomatoes, balsamic vinegar, capers and the remaining chopped garlic. Leave to cool to room temperature.

4 Put the salad in a serving bowl and sprinkle with chopped fresh parsley. Garnish with thyme, if you like, and serve at room temperature.

Nutritional information per portion: Energy 125kcal/520kJ; Protein 2.7g; Carbohydrate 11g, of which sugars 9.6g; Fat 8.1g, of which saturates 1.2g; Cholesterol 0mg; Calcium 34mg; Fibre 3.2g; Sodium 33mg.

Libyan spicy pumpkin dip

This spicy Sephardi dip from a Libyan-Jewish restaurant in Jaffa is great to serve at a Thanksgiving feast. It can be stored for at least a week in the refrigerator. Serve with raw vegetables to dip into it.

SERVES 6–8

45–60ml/3–4 tbsp olive oil
1 onion, finely chopped
5–8 garlic cloves, roughly chopped
675g/1½ lb pumpkin, peeled
   and diced
5–10ml/1–2 tsp ground cumin
5ml/1 tsp paprika
1.5–2.5ml/¼–½ tsp ground ginger
1.5–2.5ml/¼–½ tsp curry powder
75g/3oz chopped canned tomatoes
½–1 red jalapeño chilli, chopped
pinch of sugar, if necessary
juice of ½ lemon, or to taste
salt
30ml/2 tbsp chopped fresh coriander
   (cilantro) leaves, to garnish

1 Heat the oil in a frying pan, add the onion and half the garlic and fry until softened. Add the pumpkin, then cover and cook for about 10 minutes, or until half-tender.

2 Add the spices to the pan and cook for 1–2 minutes. Stir in the tomatoes, chilli, sugar and salt and cook over a medium-high heat until the liquid has evaporated completely.

3 When the pumpkin is tender, mash to a coarse purée. Add the remaining garlic and taste for seasoning, then stir in the lemon juice to taste. Serve at room temperature, sprinkled with the chopped fresh coriander.

Nutritional information per portion: Energy 54kcal/224kJ; Protein 0.9g; Carbohydrate 2.9g, of which sugars 2.3g; Fat 4.4g, of which saturates 0.7g; Cholesterol 0mg; Calcium 37mg; Fibre 1.3g; Sodium 3mg.

Smoky aubergine and pepper salad

You can also cook the aubergines and peppers under the grill until the skins blacken, if you prefer. This simple and fresh-tasting salad is delicious served with toasted slices of bread.

SERVES 4–6

2 aubergines (eggplants)
2 red (bell) peppers
3–5 garlic cloves, chopped, or to taste
2.5ml/¹⁄₂ tsp ground cumin
juice of ¹⁄₂–1 lemon, to taste
2.5ml/¹⁄₂ tsp sherry vinegar or wine
    vinegar
45–60ml/3–4 tbsp extra virgin olive oil
1–2 shakes of cayenne pepper, Tabasco or
    other hot pepper sauce
coarse sea salt
chopped fresh coriander (cilantro),
    to garnish
pitta bread wedges or toasted thinly
    sliced French bread or ciabatta bread,
    sesame seed crackers and cucumber
    slices, to serve

1 Place the aubergines and peppers directly over a medium-low gas flame or on the coals of a barbecue. Turn the vegetables frequently until deflated and the skins are evenly charred.

2 Put the aubergines and peppers in a plastic bag or in a bowl and seal tightly. Leave to cool for 30–40 minutes.

3 Peel the vegetables, reserving the juices, and roughly chop the flesh. Put the flesh in a bowl and add the juices, garlic, cumin, lemon juice, vinegar, olive oil, hot pepper seasoning and salt. Mix well to combine. Turn the mixture into a serving bowl and garnish with coriander. Serve with toast, bread, sesame seed crackers and cucumber slices.

Nutritional information per portion: Energy 74kcal/308kJ; Protein 1g; Carbohydrate 4.7g, of which sugars 4.4g; Fat 5.9g, of which saturates 0.9g; Cholesterol 0mg; Calcium 9mg; Fibre 1.8g; Sodium 3mg.

Bulgarian cucumber and walnut appetizer

Many Bulgarian Jews came to Israel bringing with them their passion for excellent yogurts, which are often used in salads. When made with thick Greek yogurt, this appetizer can be shaped into balls and served on salad leaves.

SERVES 4–6

1 large cucumber
3–5 garlic cloves, finely chopped
250ml/8fl oz/1 cup sour cream or 120ml/
    4fl oz/1/2 cup Greek (US strained plain)
    yogurt mixed with 120ml/4fl oz/1/2 cup
    double (heavy) cream
250ml/8fl oz/1 cup yogurt, preferably thick
    Greek or Bulgarian sheep's milk yogurt
30–45ml/2–3 tbsp chopped fresh dill
45–60ml/3–4 tbsp chopped walnuts
salt
sprig of dill, to garnish (optional)

1 Using a sharp knife, dice the cucumber finely, leaving the peel on, and place in a large mixing bowl.

2 Add the garlic, sour cream or yogurt and cream, yogurt, dill and salt. Mix together, then cover and chill in the refrigerator until ready to serve.

3 To serve, pile the chilled mixture into a serving bowl and sprinkle with chopped walnuts. Garnish with a sprig of dill, if you like.

Nutritional information per portion: Energy 164kcal/677kJ; Protein 4.7g; Carbohydrate 5.5g, of which sugars 5.4g; Fat 13.9g, of which saturates 5.8g; Cholesterol 26mg; Calcium 131mg; Fibre 0.5g; Sodium 53mg.

Mint and parsley tahini salad

Tahini is a creamy sesame seed paste that is widely used in Israeli and Arab cooking. Its almost dry flavour combines wonderfully with fresh herbs and subtle spices in this salad to make a light and refreshing appetizer.

SERVES 4–6

115g/4oz/1/2 cup tahini
3 garlic cloves, chopped
1/2 bunch (about 20g/3/4oz) fresh mint, chopped
1/2 bunch (about 20g/3/4oz) fresh coriander (cilantro), chopped
1/2 bunch (about 20g/3/4oz) fresh flat leaf parsley, chopped
juice of 1/2 lemon, or to taste
pinch of ground cumin
pinch of ground turmeric
pinch of ground cardamom seeds
cayenne pepper, to taste
salt
extra virgin olive oil, warmed pitta bread, olives and raw
    vegetables, to serve

1 In a bowl, or in a food processor, combine the tahini with the garlic, herbs and lemon juice. Taste and add more lemon juice, if you like. Add a little water if too thick.

2 Stir in the cumin, turmeric and cardamom to taste, then season with salt and cayenne pepper.

3 To serve, spoon into a shallow bowl or on to plates and drizzle with olive oil. Serve with warmed pitta bread, olives and raw vegetables.

Nutritional information per portion: Energy 125kcal/516kJ; Protein 4.3g; Carbohydrate 0.9g, of which sugars 0.7g; Fat 11.6g, of which saturates 1.6g; Cholesterol 0mg; Calcium 180mg; Fibre 2.8g; Sodium 12mg.

Vegetarian chopped liver

This mixture of browned onions, chopped vegetables, hard-boiled egg and walnuts looks and tastes surprisingly like chopped liver but is lighter and fresher.

SERVES 6

90ml/6 tbsp vegetable oil, plus extra if
   necessary
3 onions, chopped
175–200g/6–7oz/1¹/₂–scant 1³/₄ cups
   frozen or fresh shelled peas
115–150g/4–5oz/1 cup green beans,
   roughly chopped
15 walnuts, shelled (30 halves)
3 hard-boiled eggs, shelled
salt and ground black pepper
rye bread or crisp matzos, to serve

1 Heat the oil in a large pan, add the onions and fry until softened and lightly browned.

2 Add the peas and green beans and season to taste. Continue to cook until the beans and peas are tender and the beans are no longer bright green.

3 Put the vegetables in a food processor, add the walnuts and eggs and process until the mixture forms a thick paste.

4 Taste for seasoning and, if the mixture seems a bit dry, add a little more oil and mix in well. Serve with slices of rye bread or matzos.

Nutritional information per portion: Energy 309kcal/1277kJ; Protein 9g; Carbohydrate 11.1g, of which sugars 6.2g; Fat 25.9g, of which saturates 3.4g; Cholesterol 95mg; Calcium 64mg; Fibre 3.6g; Sodium 39mg.

Chopped chicken livers

The French love of liver-enriched pâtés is an inheritance from the Jews of Alsace, Strasbourg and the East who brought their specialities with them when they fled, and shared them at their table.

SERVES 4–6

250g/9oz chicken livers

2–3 onions, chopped, plus ½ onion, finely chopped or grated

60ml/4 tbsp rendered chicken fat or vegetable oil

3–4 spring onions (scallions), thinly sliced

2–3 hard-boiled eggs, roughly chopped or diced

10ml/2 tsp mayonnaise or firm chicken fat (optional)

5–10ml/1–2 tsp chopped fresh dill

salt and ground black pepper

chopped fresh dill or parsley, to garnish

lettuce, crisp matzos or thin slices of rye bread and dill pickles, to serve

1 Grill (broil) the livers lightly to bring the blood out on to the surface and render them kosher. Rinse, place in a pan, cover with cold water and bring to the boil. Lower the heat and simmer for 5–10 minutes, then cool in the water.

2 In a large pan, fry the onions in the fat over a medium heat, sprinkling with salt and pepper, until well browned and beginning to crisp, and caramelized around the edges.

3 Using a round-bladed knife, chop the livers finely. Place in a bowl and mix in the fried onions and oil.

4 Combine the livers with the finely chopped onion, the spring onions, eggs, mayonnaise, if using, and dill. Chill for an hour until firm.

5 Mound the chopped livers on plates and garnish with the dill or parsley. Serve with lettuce, matzos or rye bread and dill pickles.

Nutritional information per portion: Energy 180kcal/749kJ; Protein 12g; Carbohydrate 8.2g, of which sugars 5.9g; Fat 11.4g, of which saturates 1.9g; Cholesterol 253mg; Calcium 55mg; Fibre 1.8g; Sodium 72mg.

Brik a l'oeuf

These pastries are sold in the marketplaces of Israel. Men balancing full trays of briks will negotiate the crowds in a bid to sell their crispy pastries before the market closes for the long afternoon siesta. Traditionally, briks are made with a thin pastry called warka but filo pastry makes an excellent alternative.

SERVES 4

1 onion, finely chopped
30–45ml/2–3 tbsp chopped
   fresh parsley or coriander
   (cilantro), or a mixture
   of both
a pinch of chopped fresh
   chilli (optional)
4 filo pastry sheets
90–115g/3¹/₂–4oz can tuna,
   well drained
vegetable oil, for deep-frying
4 eggs
hot sauce, such as zchug, harissa
   or Tabasco, to serve

1 In a bowl, combine the onion, herbs and chilli, if using. Lay a sheet of pastry on some baking parchment. Put one-quarter of the onion mixture at one corner, then add one-quarter of the tuna.

2 Preheat the oven to 200°C/400°F/Gas 6. Heat the oil in a pan until it browns a cube of bread in 30 seconds.

3 Break an egg into a bowl, then put it into the corner of the pastry sheet with the onion. Fold over the pastry to form a triangle and enclose the egg. Fry the parcel until golden brown. Remove with a slotted spoon, drain on kitchen paper, then transfer to a baking sheet. Make three more pastries.

4 Bake the pastries for 5 minutes, or until crisp and golden brown. Do not overcook as the egg yolk must be runny. Serve with hot sauce for dipping.

Nutritional information per portion: Energy 267kcal/1111kJ; Protein 14.1g; Carbohydrate 11.2g, of which sugars 1.3g; Fat 18.9g, of which saturates 3.2g; Cholesterol 202mg; Calcium 75mg; Fibre 1.2g; Sodium 140mg.

Rebecchine de Jerusalemme

These stuffed polenta fritters come from the Jewish community of Italy. Polenta, cooked to a thick consistency and poured out to cool into a firm bread-like mixture, is the "bread" of these tiny fried sandwiches. Anchovies are the traditional filling but here a little tomato, rosemary and cheese have been used. Porcini mushrooms also make a good filling.

SERVES 6

250g/9oz/1½ cups polenta
30–45ml/2–3 tbsp tomato purée (paste)
30–45ml/2–3 tbsp diced ripe fresh or
    canned chopped tomatoes
30ml/2 tbsp chopped fresh rosemary
30–45ml/2–3 tbsp freshly grated
    Parmesan or Pecorino cheese
130g/4½oz mozzarella, Gorgonzola or
    fontina cheese, finely chopped
half vegetable and half olive oil,
    for frying
1–2 eggs, lightly beaten
plain (all-purpose) flour, for dusting
salt
diced red (bell) pepper, shredded lettuce
    and rosemary sprigs, to garnish

1 In a large pan, combine the polenta with 250ml/8fl oz/1 cup cold water and stir. Add 750ml/1¼ pints/3 cups boiling water, bring to the boil and cook, stirring, for 30 minutes until the mixture is thick and no longer grainy. Season. Pour into an oiled baking dish, forming a layer 1cm/½in thick. Chill.

2 Using a 6–7.5cm/2½–3in plain pastry (cookie) cutter, cut the polenta into rounds. Combine the tomato purée with the tomatoes. Spread a little of the mixture on the soft, moist side of a polenta round, sprinkle with rosemary and a little cheese, then top with another round of polenta. Press the edges together. Fill the remaining polenta rounds in the same way.

3 Pour a 5cm/2in depth of oil into a large frying pan, and heat until hot enough to brown a cube of bread in 30 seconds. Dip a sandwich into the egg, then coat in the flour. Fry for 4–5 minutes, turning once. Drain and cook the remaining polentas in the same way. Garnish with pepper, lettuce and rosemary.

Nutritional information per portion: Energy 333kcal/1386kJ; Protein 11.4g; Carbohydrate 31.8g, of which sugars 1.3g; Fat 17.5g, of which saturates 5.3g; Cholesterol 49mg; Calcium 148mg; Fibre 1.2g; Sodium 171mg.

Herring salad with beetroot and sour cream

This salad, served with black pumpernickel bread, is the quintessential Shabbat morning dish after services. Serve with cold boiled potatoes and allow your guests to add to the salad as they like.

SERVES 8

1 large tangy cooking apple

500g/1¼lb mates herrings (schmaltz herrings), drained and cut into slices

2 small pickled cucumbers, diced

10ml/2 tsp caster (superfine) sugar, or to taste

10ml/2 tsp cider vinegar or white wine vinegar

300ml/½ pint/1¼ cups sour cream

2 cooked beetroot (beets), diced

lettuce, to serve

sprigs of fresh dill and chopped onion or onion rings, to garnish

1 Peel, core and dice the apple. Put in a bowl, add the herrings, cucumbers, sugar and vinegar and mix together. Add the sour cream and mix well to combine.

2 Add the beetroot to the herring mixture and chill in the refrigerator. Serve the salad on a bed of lettuce leaves, garnished with fresh dill and chopped onion or onion rings.

Nutritional information per portion: Energy 212kcal/878kJ; Protein 9.6g; Carbohydrate 6.5g, of which sugars 6.2g; Fat 16.5g, of which saturates 4.7g; Cholesterol 51mg; Calcium 72mg; Fibre 0.6g; Sodium 266mg.

Mushroom caviar on garlic-rubbed rye toasts

Mixtures of finely chopped vegetables are very popular in the Jewish kitchen. The name caviar simply refers to the dark colour and rich texture, rather than the actual content, of the dish.

SERVES 4

10–15g /1/4–1/2oz dried porcini or other
    well-flavoured dried mushrooms
120ml/4fl oz /1/2 cup water
45ml/3 tbsp olive or vegetable oil
450g/1lb mushrooms, roughly chopped
5–10 shallots, chopped
5 garlic cloves, 4 chopped and 1 whole
30ml/2 tbsp port
juice of 1/4 lemon, or to taste
12–16 slices cocktail rye bread or
    2 ordinary slices, cut in halves
salt
2–3 spring onions (scallions), thinly
    shredded, and/or 15ml/1 tbsp chopped
    fresh parsley, and 1 chopped hard-
    boiled egg, or sour cream, to garnish

1 Soak the dried mushrooms in the water for about 30 minutes.

2 Heat the oil in a pan, add the fresh mushrooms, shallots and chopped garlic and fry until browned. Season with salt.

3 Add the soaked mushrooms and water and cook until all the liquid has evaporated. Add the port and lemon juice and continue cooking until they have evaporated and the mixture is brown and dry.

4 Put the mixture in a food processor and process briefly until a chunky paste is formed.

5 Toast the rye bread until golden on both sides, then rub with the whole garlic clove.

6 Carefully spoon the mushroom caviar into individual dishes and serve with the toast and garnished with the spring onions, chopped parsley, and hard-boiled egg, or sour cream.

Nutritional information per portion: Energy 143kcal/596kJ; Protein 3.7g; Carbohydrate 10.3g, of which sugars 3.7g; Fat 9.1g, of which saturates 1.1g; Cholesterol 0mg; Calcium 29mg; Fibre 2.4g; Sodium 80mg.

Chopped egg and onions

This Ashkenazi dish, although the essence of modern Western deli food, is in fact one of the oldest dishes in Jewish history. Some say that it goes back to Egyptian times. It is delicious piled on to toast or used as a sandwich or bagel filling.

SERVES 4–6

8–10 eggs
6–8 spring onions (scallions) and/or 1 yellow or white onion,
    very finely chopped, plus extra to garnish
60–90ml/4–6 tbsp mayonnaise or rendered chicken fat
mild French wholegrain mustard, to taste (optional if using
    mayonnaise)
15ml/1 tbsp chopped fresh parsley
salt and ground black pepper
rye toasts or crackers, to serve

1 Put the eggs in a large pan and cover with cold water. Bring the water to the boil and when it boils, reduce the heat and simmer over a low heat for 10 minutes.

2 Hold the eggs under cold running water, then remove the shells, dry the eggs and chop roughly.

3 Place the chopped eggs in a large bowl, add the onions, season generously with salt and pepper and mix well. Add enough mayonnaise or chicken fat to bind the mixture together. Stir in the mustard, if using, and the chopped parsley, or sprinkle the parsley on top to garnish. Chill before serving with rye toasts or crackers.

Nutritional information per portion: Energy 197kcal/816kJ; Protein 11g; Carbohydrate 0.7g, of which sugars 0.6g; Fat 17g, of which saturates 3.7g; Cholesterol 325mg; Calcium 69mg; Fibre 0.6g; Sodium 165mg.

Israeli white cheese and green olives

The dairy shelves of Israel boast an ever-increasing array of cheeses, from kashkaval to goat's cheeses and mild white cheeses spiked with seasonings such as this one with piquant green olives. Serve with drinks and crackers, or as a brunch spread with bread or bagels.

SERVES 4

175–200g/6–7oz soft white
    (farmer's) cheese
65g/2¹/₂ oz feta cheese, preferably sheep's milk,
    lightly crumbled
20–30 pitted green olives, some chopped, the rest halved
    or quartered
2–3 large pinches of fresh thyme,
    plus extra to garnish
2–3 garlic cloves, finely chopped (optional)
crackers, toast or bagels, to serve

1 Place the soft cheese in a bowl and stir with the back of a spoon until soft and smooth.

2 Add the crumbled feta cheese to the blended soft cheese and stir until thoroughly combined.

3 Add the olives, thyme and chopped garlic to the cheese mixture and mix well to combine.

4 Spoon the mixture into a bowl, sprinkle with thyme and serve with crackers, toast, chunks of bread or bagels.

Nutritional information per portion: Energy 242kcal/1002kJ; Protein 13.8g; Carbohydrate 0.3g, of which sugars 0.3g; Fat 19.7g, of which saturates 12g; Cholesterol 54mg; Calcium 393mg; Fibre 0.6g; Sodium 972mg.

Sweet and sour red cabbage

Cabbage used to be the most important vegetable in the Ashkenazi kitchen and often it was the only vegetable. Luckily cabbage is very versatile and is also very good for you. This dish can be made ahead of time and reheated at the last minute to serve with either a meat or dairy meal.

SERVES 4–6

30ml/2 tbsp vegetable oil
1/2 large or 1 small red
    cabbage, cored and
    thinly sliced
1 large onion, chopped
2–3 handfuls of raisins
1 small apple, finely diced
15ml/1 tbsp sugar
120ml/4fl oz/1/2 cup dry red wine
juice of 1 lemon or 50ml/2fl oz/
    1/4 cup lemon juice and cider vinegar
    mixed together
salt and ground black pepper

1 Heat the oil in a large pan, add the cabbage and onion and fry for 3–5 minutes, stirring, until the vegetables are well coated in the oil and the cabbage has softened slightly.

2 Add the raisins, apple, sugar and red wine and cook for 30 minutes, or until very tender.

3 Check the cabbage occasionally and add more water or red wine if the liquid has evaporated and the cabbage is at risk of burning.

4 Towards the end of the cooking time, add the lemon juice, and vinegar if using, and season with salt and pepper to taste. Serve the cabbage hot or cold.

Nutritional information per portion: Energy 148kcal/620kJ; Protein 2.2g; Carbohydrate 23.8g, of which sugars 22.2g; Fat 4g, of which saturates 0.4g; Cholesterol 0mg; Calcium 60mg; Fibre 2.9g; Sodium 19mg.

Sweet and sour cucumber with fresh dill

This is half pickle, half salad, and totally delicious served as a light brunch or even as an appetizer before a homely, roasted meat main course. Serve with thin slices of pumpernickel or any other coarse, dark, full-flavoured bread.

SERVES 4

1 large or 2 small cucumbers, thinly sliced
3 onions, thinly sliced
45ml/3 tbsp sugar
75–90ml/5–6 tbsp white wine vinegar
**   or cider vinegar**
30–45ml/2–3 tbsp water
30–45ml/2–3 tbsp chopped fresh dill
salt

1 In a large bowl, mix together the sliced cucumber and onions, season with salt and toss together until thoroughly combined. Leave to stand in a cool place for about 5–10 minutes.

2 Add the sugar, vinegar, water and chopped dill to the cucumber mixture. Toss together until well combined, then chill in the refrigerator for a few hours, or until ready to serve.

Nutritional information per portion: Energy 89kcal/375kJ; Protein 2g; Carbohydrate 20.7g, of which sugars 18.3g; Fat 0.4g, of which saturates 0g; Cholesterol 0mg; Calcium 63mg; Fibre 2.3g; Sodium 9mg.

New York deli coleslaw

Every deli sells coleslaw but there is boring coleslaw and exciting coleslaw. The key to good coleslaw is a zesty dressing and an interesting selection of vegetables.

SERVES 6–8

1 large white or green cabbage, very thinly sliced
3–4 carrots, coarsely grated
1/2 red (bell) pepper, chopped
1/2 green (bell) pepper, chopped
1–2 celery sticks, finely chopped, or 5–10ml/1–2 tsp celery seeds
1 onion, chopped
2–3 handfuls of raisins or sultanas (golden raisins)
45ml/3 tbsp white wine vinegar or
    cider vinegar
60–90ml/4–6 tbsp sugar, to taste
175–250ml/6–8fl oz/3/4–1 cup mayonnaise, to bind
salt and ground black pepper

1 Put the cabbage, carrots, peppers, celery or celery seeds, onion, and raisins or sultanas in a large salad bowl and mix to combine well. Add the vinegar, sugar, salt and ground black pepper and toss together. Cover and leave to stand for about 1 hour.

2 Stir enough mayonnaise into the salad to lightly bind the ingredients together. Taste the salad for seasoning and sweet-and-sour flavour, adding more sugar, salt and pepper if needed.

3 Chill in the refrigerator until ready to serve and drain off any excess liquid before serving.

Nutritional information per portion: Energy 215kcal/891kJ; Protein 1.6g; Carbohydrate 15.1g, of which sugars 14.6g; Fat 16.8g, of which saturates 2.6g; Cholesterol 16mg; Calcium 46mg; Fibre 2.3g; Sodium 115mg.

Deli potato salad

Potato salad is synonymous with deli food and there are many varieties, some with sour cream and some with vinaigrette. This version includes a mustard mayonnaise and olives.

SERVES 6–8

1kg/2 1/4lb waxy salad potatoes, scrubbed
1 red, brown or white onion, finely chopped
2–3 celery sticks, finely chopped
60–90ml/4–6 tbsp chopped fresh parsley
15–20 pimiento-stuffed olives, halved
3 hard-boiled eggs, chopped
60ml/4 tbsp extra virgin olive oil
60ml/4 tbsp white wine vinegar
15–30ml/1–2 tbsp mild or wholegrain mustard
celery seeds, to taste (optional)
175–250ml/6–8fl oz/3/4–1 cup mayonnaise
salt and ground black pepper
paprika, to garnish

1 Cook the potatoes in a pan of salted boiling water until tender. Drain, return to the pan and leave for 2–3 minutes to cool and dry a little.

2 When the potatoes are cool enough to handle but still very warm, cut them into chunks and place in a bowl. Season, then add the onion, celery, parsley, olives and the chopped eggs.

3 Combine the olive oil, vinegar, mustard and celery seeds, if using, pour over the salad and toss to combine. Add enough mayonnaise to bind the salad together. Chill before serving, sprinkled with a little paprika.

Nutritional information per portion: Energy 323kcal/1343kJ; Protein 5.2g; Carbohydrate 21.5g, of which sugars 2.7g; Fat 24.7g, of which saturates 4g; Cholesterol 88mg; Calcium 49mg; Fibre 2g; Sodium 149mg.

Whitefish salad

Smoked whitefish is one of the glories of deli food and, made into a salad with mayonnaise and sour cream, it becomes indispensable as a brunch dish. Serve it with a stack of bagels, pumpernickel or rye bread. If you can't find smoked whitefish, you can use any other smoked firm white fish such as halibut or cod.

SERVES 4–6

1 smoked whitefish, skinned
    and boned
2 celery sticks, chopped
1/2 red, white or yellow onion
    or 3–5 spring onions
    (scallions), chopped
45ml/3 tbsp mayonnaise
45ml/3 tbsp sour cream or Greek
    (US strained plain) yogurt
juice of 1/2–1 lemon
1 round lettuce
ground black pepper
5–10ml/1–2 tsp chopped fresh parsley,
    to garnish

1 Break the smoked fish into bitesize pieces. In a bowl, combine the chopped celery, onion or spring onions, mayonnaise, and sour cream or yogurt, and add lemon juice to taste.

2 Fold the fish into the mixture and season with pepper. Arrange the lettuce leaves on serving plates, then spoon the whitefish salad on top. Serve chilled, sprinkled with parsley.

Nutritional information per portion: Energy 112kcal/469kJ; Protein 10.1g; Carbohydrate 1g, of which sugars 1g; Fat 7.6g, of which saturates 1.9g; Cholesterol 28mg; Calcium 29mg; Fibre 0.3g; Sodium 421mg.

Marinated herrings

This is a classic Ashkenazi dish, sweet-and-sour and lightly spiced. It is delicious for Sunday brunch and is always welcomed at a Shabbat midday kiddush reception. This dish is best made two days before you need to serve it so all the flavours are allowed to develop. Serve with some rye or pumpernickel bread.

SERVES 4–6

2–3 herrings, filleted
1 onion, sliced
juice of 1¹/₂ lemons
30ml/2 tbsp white wine vinegar
25ml/1¹/₂ tbsp sugar
10–15 black peppercorns
10–15 allspice berries
1.5ml/¹/₄ tsp mustard seeds
3 bay leaves, torn
salt

1 Soak the herrings in cold water for 5 minutes, then drain. Pour over water to cover and soak for 2–3 hours, then drain. Pour over water to cover and leave to soak overnight.

2 Hold the soaked herrings under cold running water and rinse very well, both inside and out. Cut each fish into bitesize pieces, then place the pieces in a glass bowl or shallow dish.

3 Sprinkle the onion over the fish, then add the lemon juice, vinegar, sugar, peppercorns, allspice, mustard seeds, bay leaves and salt. Add enough water to just cover. Chill for 2 days to let the flavours blend before serving.

Nutritional information per portion: Energy 94kcal/393kJ; Protein 7.7g; Carbohydrate 3.4g, of which sugars 3.2g; Fat 5.6g, of which saturates 1.4g; Cholesterol 21mg; Calcium 29mg; Fibre 0.1g; Sodium 52mg.

Scrambled eggs with lox and onions

Serve this quintessential New York Sunday brunch with piles of freshly toasted bagels, mugs of coffee and a selection of Sunday newspapers.

SERVES 4

40g/1½oz/3 tbsp unsalted (sweet) butter

2 onions, chopped

150–200g/5–7oz smoked salmon

6–8 eggs, lightly beaten

ground black pepper

45ml/3 tbsp chopped fresh chives, plus whole chives, to garnish

bagels, to serve

1 Heat half the unsalted butter in a large frying pan, add the chopped onions and fry until softened and just beginning to brown. Add the smoked salmon to the onions and mix well until everything is combined.

2 Pour the eggs into the pan and stir until soft curds form. Add the remaining butter and stir off the heat until creamy. Season with pepper. Spoon on to serving plates and garnish with chives. Serve with bagels.

Nutritional information per portion: Energy 288kcal/1199kJ; Protein 22.5g; Carbohydrate 3g, of which sugars 2.2g; Fat 21.1g, of which saturates 8.6g; Cholesterol 415mg; Calcium 75mg; Fibre 0.5g; Sodium 907mg.

Matzo brei

Every Ashkenazi family has its own version of this dish of soaked matzos, mixed with egg and fried until crisp. This version is crisp, salty and broken into pieces.

SERVES 1

3 matzos, broken into bitesize pieces
2 eggs, lightly beaten
30–45ml/2–3 tbsp olive oil or
    25–40g/1–1½ oz/2–3 tbsp butter
salt
sour cream and fresh dill,
    to serve (optional)

1 Put the matzos in a large bowl and pour over cold water to cover. Leave for 2–3 minutes, then drain. Add the eggs.

2 Heat the oil or butter in a frying pan, then add the matzo mixture. Lower the heat and cook for 2–3 minutes until the bottom is golden brown.

3 Break up the matzo brei into pieces, turn them over and brown their other side. Turn once or twice again until the pieces are crisp. (The more times you turn them, the smaller the pieces will become.)

4 Sprinkle with a little salt and serve immediately, with sour cream and dill if you like.

Nutritional information per portion: Energy 554kcal/2296kJ; Protein 15.2g; Carbohydrate 19g, of which sugars 0.6g; Fat 47.2g, of which saturates 7.8g; Cholesterol 381mg; Calcium 87mg; Fibre 0.8g; Sodium 258mg.

Kasha and mushroom knishes

Made in tiny, one-bite pastries, knishes are delicious cocktail or appetizer fare; made in big, handful-sized pastries they are the perfect accompaniment to a large bowl of borscht.

MAKES ABOUT 15

40g/1¹/₂oz/3 tbsp butter (for a dairy
    meal), 45ml/3 tbsp rendered chicken
    or duck fat (for a meat meal), or
    vegetable oil (for a pareve filling)
2 onions, finely chopped
200g/7oz/scant 3 cups mushrooms, diced
    (optional)
200–250g/7–9oz/1–1¹/₄
    cups buckwheat, cooked
handful of mixed dried mushrooms,
    broken into small pieces
200ml/7fl oz/scant 1 cup hot stock,
    preferably mushroom
1 egg, lightly beaten
salt and ground black pepper

FOR THE SOUR CREAM PASTRY
250g/9oz/2¹/₄ cups plain
    (all-purpose) flour
5ml/1 tsp baking powder
2.5ml/¹/₂ tsp salt
2.5ml/¹/₂ tsp sugar
130g/4¹/₂oz/generous ¹/₂ cup plus
    15ml/1 tbsp unsalted (sweet) butter,
    cut into small pieces
75g/3oz sour cream or Greek
    (US strained plain) yogurt

1 To make the pastry, sift together the flour, baking powder, salt and sugar, then rub in the butter until the mixture resembles fine breadcrumbs.

2 Add the sour cream or yogurt and mix together to form a dough. Add 5ml/1 tsp water if necessary. Wrap the dough in a plastic bag and chill for about 2 hours.

3 To make the filling, heat the butter, fat or oil in a pan, add the onions and fresh mushrooms, if using, and fry until soft and browned. Add the buckwheat and cook until slightly browned. Add the dried mushrooms and stock and cook over a medium-high heat until the liquid has been absorbed. Leave to cool, then stir in the egg and season well.

4 Preheat the oven to 200°C/400°F/Gas 6. Roll out the pastry on a lightly floured surface to about 3mm/¹/₈in thickness, then cut into rectangles (about 7.5 x 16cm/3 x 6¹/₄in). Place 2–3 spoonfuls of the filling in the middle of each piece and brush the edges with water, fold up and pinch together to seal. Bake for 15 minutes.

Nutritional information per pastry: Energy 210kcal/876kJ; Protein 3.6g; Carbohydrate 22.7g, of which sugars 2.4g; Fat 12.3g, of which saturates 7.4g; Cholesterol 43mg; Calcium 44mg; Fibre 1.1g; Sodium 86mg.

Fish dishes

Fish is pareve (neutral) and so may be

eaten with either meat or dairy foods. This

provides variety and flexibility within the

otherwise demanding laws of Kashrut.

Both Ashkenazim and Sephardim have

many traditional fish dishes, from Peruvian

fried whitebait to whole fish baked with

fragrant spices from Israel.

Baked salmon with watercress sauce

Whole baked salmon is a classic dish served at Bar and Bat Mitzvah feasts, wedding parties and any big simcha, or festival. Baking the salmon in foil produces a flesh rather like that of a poached fish but with the ease of baking. Decorating the fish with thin slices of cucumber looks pretty and will conceal any flesh that may look ragged after skinning.

SERVES 6-8

2-3kg/4¹/₂-6³/₄lb salmon,
   cleaned with head and tail
   left on
3-5 spring onions (scallions),
   thinly sliced
1 lemon, thinly sliced
1 cucumber, thinly sliced
fresh dill sprigs, to garnish
lemon wedges, to serve

FOR THE WATERCRESS SAUCE

3 garlic cloves, chopped
200g/7oz watercress leaves, chopped
40g/1¹/₂oz fresh tarragon, chopped
300ml/¹/₂ pint/1¹/₄ cups mayonnaise
15-30ml/1-2 tbsp freshly squeezed
   lemon juice
200g/7oz/scant 1 cup butter
salt and ground black pepper

1 Preheat the oven to 180°C/350°F/Gas 4. Rinse the salmon and lay it on a large piece of foil. Stuff the fish with the sliced spring onions and layer the lemon slices inside and around the fish, then season.

2 Loosely fold the foil around the fish and fold the edges over to seal. Bake for 1 hour. Let the fish stand, still in the foil, for 15 minutes, then unwrap and leave to cool.

3 When the fish is cool, lift it on to a large plate, still covered with lemon slices. Cover tightly with clear film (plastic wrap) and chill for several hours.

4 Before serving, discard the lemon slices around the fish. Using a blunt knife to lift up the edge of the skin, peel the skin away from the flesh and pull out any fins. Arrange the cucumber slices in overlapping rows along the length of the fish, to resemble large fish scales.

5 For the sauce, put the garlic, watercress, tarragon, mayonnaise and lemon juice in a food processor or bowl and process or mix to combine. Melt the butter, then add to the watercress mixture, a little at a time, until the butter has been incorporated and the sauce is smooth. Cover and chill before serving, garnished with dill, with the sauce and lemon wedges.

Nutritional information per portion: Energy 515kcal/2133kJ; Protein 25.5g; Carbohydrate 0.7g, of which sugars 0.6g; Fat 45.6g, of which saturates 14g; Cholesterol 114mg; Calcium 67mg; Fibre 0.4g; Sodium 275mg.

Classic Ashkenazi gefilte fish

Gefilte means stuffed and originally this mixture of chopped fish was carefully stuffed back into the skin of the fish before cooking. These fishballs are served at the start of most Jewish festivities.

SERVES 8

1kg/2¼lb of 2–3 varieties of fish fillets, such as carp, whitefish, yellow pike, haddock and cod
2 eggs
120ml/4fl oz/½ cup cold water
30–45ml/2–3 tbsp medium matzo meal
15–45ml/1–3 tbsp sugar
fish stock, for simmering
2–3 onions
3 carrots
1–2 pinches of ground cinnamon
salt and ground black pepper
chrain or horseradish and beetroot (beet) pickle, to serve

1 Sprinkle the fish with salt and chill for 1 hour, or until the flesh has firmed. Rinse, then process in a food processor until minced (ground).

2 Put the fish into a bowl, add the eggs, mix, then gradually add the water. Stir in the matzo meal, then the sugar and seasoning. Beat until light, then chill for 1 hour.

3 Take 15–30ml/1–2 tbsp of the mixture and, with wet hands, roll into a ball. Continue with the remaining mixture.

4 Bring a pan of fish stock to the boil, lower the heat to a simmer and add the fishballs. Return to the boil, lower the heat and simmer for 1 hour. Add more water, if necessary, to keep covered.

5 Add the onions, carrots, cinnamon and a little sugar, if you like, to the pan and simmer, uncovered, for 45–60 minutes.

6 Leave to cool slightly, then remove from the liquid. Serve warm or cold with horseradish and beetroot pickle.

Nutritional information per portion: Energy 159kcal/667kJ; Protein 25.5g; Carbohydrate 8.7g, of which sugars 4.7g; Fat 2.6g, of which saturates 0.5g; Cholesterol 105mg; Calcium 37mg; Fibre 1.4g; Sodium 100mg.

Ginger fishballs in tomato and lemon sauce

If you cannot find preserved lemon then you can always use a fresh lemon. Just cut the lemon into small dice and add it with the tomatoes. You can use cod, haddock or whiting for this dish.

SERVES 6

65g/2¹/₂oz bread (about 2 slices)
1kg/2¹/₄lb minced (ground) white fish
2 onions, chopped
8 garlic cloves, chopped
2.5–5ml/¹/₂–1 tsp ground turmeric
2.5ml/¹/₂ tsp ground ginger
2.5ml/¹/₂ tsp garam masala
1 bunch fresh coriander (cilantro),
    chopped, plus extra to garnish
1 egg
cayenne pepper, to taste
150ml/¹/₄ pint/²/₃ cup vegetable oil
4 ripe tomatoes, diced
5ml/1 tsp paprika
1 preserved lemon, rinsed and cut into
    small strips
salt and ground black pepper
¹/₂ lemon, cut into wedges, to serve

1 Remove the crusts from the bread, soak in a bowl of cold water for 10 minutes, then squeeze dry.

2 Add the fish to the bread with half the onions, half the garlic, half the turmeric, the ginger, half the garam masala, half the coriander, the egg and cayenne. Mix and leave to chill.

3 For the sauce, heat the oil, add the remaining onion and garlic and fry for 5 minutes, or until softened. Add the remaining turmeric and garam masala and warm through.

4 Add the diced tomatoes, paprika and remaining coriander to the pan and cook over a medium heat until the tomatoes have formed a sauce consistency. Stir in the preserved lemon.

5 With wet hands, roll walnut-size lumps of the fish mixture into balls and flatten slightly. Place in the sauce. Cook gently, for 20 minutes, turning twice. Garnish with coriander leaves and serve immediately with lemon wedges for squeezing.

Nutritional information per portion: Energy 359kcal/1496kJ; Protein 33.8g; Carbohydrate 13g, of which sugars 5.7g; Fat 19.3g, of which saturates 2.9g; Cholesterol 108mg; Calcium 55mg; Fibre 1.7g; Sodium 181mg.

Tonno con piselli

This Jewish Italian dish of fresh tuna and peas is especially enjoyed at Pesach, which falls in spring. Before the days of the freezer, spring was the time for little seasonal peas.

SERVES 4

60ml/4 tbsp olive oil

1 onion, chopped

4–5 garlic cloves, chopped

45ml/3 tbsp chopped fresh flat
    leaf parsley

1–2 pinches of fennel seeds

350g/12oz tuna steaks

400g/14oz can chopped tomatoes

120ml/4fl oz/¹⁄₂ cup dry white wine or
    fish stock

30–45ml/2–3 tbsp tomato
    purée (paste)

pinch of sugar, if needed

350g/12oz/3 cups fresh shelled or frozen
    peas

salt and ground black pepper

1 Preheat the oven to 190°C/375°F/Gas 5. Heat the olive oil in a large frying pan, then add the chopped onion, garlic, parsley and fennel seeds, and fry over a low heat for 5 minutes, or until the onion is softened but not browned.

2 Season the tuna on each side and fry for 2–3 minutes on each side until lightly browned. Transfer the tuna to a shallow baking dish, in a single layer.

3 Add the canned tomatoes along with their juice and the wine or fish stock to the onions and cook over a medium heat for 5–10 minutes, stirring, until the flavours blend together and the mixture thickens slightly.

4 Stir the tomato purée, sugar, if needed, and salt and pepper, into the tomato sauce, then add the peas. Pour over the fish steaks and bake, uncovered, for about 10 minutes, or until tender. Serve hot.

Nutritional information per portion: Energy 339kcal/1411kJ; Protein 28.1g; Carbohydrate 15.4g, of which sugars 7.2g; Fat 16.7g, of which saturates 3g; Cholesterol 25mg; Calcium 49mg; Fibre 5.5g; Sodium 71mg.

Yemenite poached fish in spicy tomato sauce

This dish is quick and easy to make and can be served as a main course or as a part of a celebratory meal. If you don't have any fresh red chillies then add one or two teaspoons of chilli paste instead.

SERVES 8

300ml/¹/₂ pint/1¹/₄ cups passata
   (bottled strained tomatoes)
150ml/¹/₄ pint/²/₃ cup fish stock
1 large onion, chopped
60ml/4 tbsp each chopped fresh
   coriander (cilantro) and parsley leaves
5–8 garlic cloves, crushed
chopped fresh red chilli, to taste
large pinch of ground ginger
large pinch of curry powder
1.5ml/¹/₄ tsp ground cumin
1.5ml/¹/₄ tsp ground turmeric
seeds from 2–3 cardamom pods
juice of 2 lemons, or to taste
30ml/2 tbsp vegetable or olive oil
1.5kg/3¹/₄lb mixed white fish fillets

1 Put the passata, stock, onion, herbs, garlic, chilli, ginger, curry powder, cumin, turmeric, cardamom, lemon juice and oil in a large pan and bring to the boil.

2 Remove from the heat and add the fish fillets to the hot sauce. Return to the heat and allow the sauce to boil briefly again. Reduce the heat and simmer very gently for about 5 minutes, or until the fish is tender. (Test the fish with a fork. If the flesh flakes easily, then it is cooked.)

3 Taste the sauce and adjust the seasoning, adding more lemon juice if necessary. Serve hot or warm, with bread.

Nutritional information per portion: Energy 191kcal/803kJ; Protein 35.1g; Carbohydrate 3.3g, of which sugars 2.7g; Fat 4.2g, of which saturates 0.5g; Cholesterol 86mg; Calcium 39mg; Fibre 0.9g; Sodium 202mg.

Peruvian whitebait escabeche

Any type of tiny white fish, fried, then marinated with vegetables, is a favourite food in Peru, especially among the Jews. Serve these tangy morsels as an appetizer with drinks or as a main course with a salad of cold mashed potatoes dressed with onions, chillies and lemon juice.

SERVES 4

800g/1³/₄lb whitebait or tiny white fish

juice of 2 lemons

5ml/1 tsp salt

plain (all-purpose) flour, for dusting

vegetable oil, for frying

2 onions, chopped or thinly sliced

2.5–5ml/¹/₂–1 tsp cumin seeds

2 carrots, thinly sliced

2 jalapeño chillies, chopped

8 garlic cloves, roughly chopped

120ml/4fl oz/¹/₂ cup white wine vinegar

2–3 large pinches of dried oregano

15–30ml/1–2 tbsp chopped fresh
    coriander (cilantro) leaves

corn on the cob, olives and coriander
    (cilantro), to garnish

1 Put the fish in a bowl, add the lemon juice and salt and leave to marinate for 30–60 minutes. Remove the fish and dust with flour.

2 Heat the oil in a deep frying pan until hot enough to turn a cube of bread golden brown in 30 seconds. Fry the fish, in small batches, until golden brown, then put in a shallow serving dish and set aside.

3 In a separate pan, heat 30ml/2 tbsp of oil. Add the onions, cumin seeds, carrots, chillies and garlic and fry for 5 minutes. Add the vinegar, oregano and coriander, stir well and cook for 1–2 minutes. Pour the onion mixture over the fish and leave to cool. Serve, garnished with slices of corn on the cob, olives and coriander leaves.

Nutritional information per portion: Energy 1087kcal/4504kJ; Protein 40.3g; Carbohydrate 18.5g, of which sugars 5.9g; Fat 95.3g, of which saturates 8.9g; Cholesterol 0mg; Calcium 1743mg; Fibre 2.3g; Sodium 471mg.

Filo-wrapped fish

This delicious dish comes from Jerusalem, where whole fish are wrapped in filo pastry and served with a zesty tomato sauce. The choice of fish can be varied according to what is in season and what is freshest on the day of purchase.

SERVES 3–4

450g/1lb salmon or cod steaks or fillets
1 lemon
30ml/2 tbsp olive oil, plus extra
    for brushing
1 onion, chopped
2 celery sticks, chopped
1 green (bell) pepper, diced
5 garlic cloves, chopped
400g/14oz canned tomatoes, chopped
120ml/4fl oz/1/2 cup passata
    (bottled strained tomatoes)
30ml/2 tbsp chopped fresh parsley
2–3 pinches of ground allspice
cayenne pepper, to taste
pinch of sugar
130g/4 1/2oz filo pastry (6–8 large sheets)
salt and ground black pepper

1 Sprinkle the salmon or cod with salt and black pepper and a squeeze of lemon juice. Set aside while you prepare the sauce.

2 Heat the oil in a pan, add the onion, celery and pepper and fry for 5 minutes. Add the garlic and cook for 1 minute, then add the tomatoes and passata and cook until the tomatoes are of a sauce consistency. Stir in the parsley, then season with allspice, cayenne pepper, sugar and salt and pepper.

3 Preheat the oven to 200°C/400°F/Gas 6. Take a sheet of filo pastry, brush with oil and cover with a second sheet. Place a piece of fish on top, towards the bottom edge, then top with 1–2 spoonfuls of the sauce, spreading it evenly. Roll the fish in the pastry. Arrange on a baking sheet and repeat.

4 Bake for 10–15 minutes, or until golden. Meanwhile, reheat the remaining sauce if necessary. Serve immediately with the remaining sauce.

Nutritional information per portion: Energy 233kcal/972kJ; Protein 18.4g; Carbohydrate 9.1g, of which sugars 2.2g; Fat 14g, of which saturates 8.2g; Cholesterol 84mg; Calcium 170mg; Fibre 1.7g; Sodium 213mg.

Moroccan grilled fish brochettes

Serve these delicious skewers with potatoes, aubergine slices and strips of red peppers, which can be cooked on the barbecue alongside the fish brochettes. Accompany with a bowl of zchug and a stack of warm, soft pitta breads or flour tortillas.

SERVES 4–6

5 garlic cloves, chopped
2.5ml/¹/₂ tsp paprika
2.5ml/¹/₂ tsp ground cumin
2.5–5ml/¹/₂–1 tsp salt
2–3 pinches of cayenne pepper
60ml/4 tbsp olive oil
30ml/2 tbsp lemon juice
30ml/2 tbsp chopped coriander (cilantro)

675g/1¹/₂lb firm-fleshed white fish, such as haddock, halibut, sea bass, snapper or turbot, cut into 2.5–5cm/1–2in cubes
3–4 green or red (bell) peppers, seeded and cut into 2.5–5cm/1–2in pieces
lemon wedges, to serve

1 Put the garlic, paprika, cumin, salt, cayenne pepper, oil, lemon juice and coriander in a large bowl and mix together. Add the fish and toss to coat. Leave to marinate for at least 30 minutes, and preferably 2 hours, at room temperature, or chill overnight.

2 About 40 minutes before you are going to cook the brochettes, light the barbecue. The barbecue is ready when the coals have turned white and grey.

3 Meanwhile, thread the fish cubes and pepper pieces alternately on to several presoaked wooden or metal skewers.

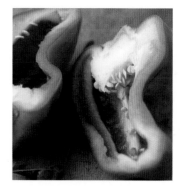

4 Grill (broil) the brochettes on the barbecue for 2–3 minutes on each side, or until the fish is tender and lightly browned. Serve with lemon wedges.

Nutritional information per portion: Energy 276kcal/1157kJ; Protein 33.3g; Carbohydrate 8g, of which sugars 7.6g; Fat 12.5g, of which saturates 1.9g; Cholesterol 61mg; Calcium 34mg; Fibre 2g; Sodium 118mg.

Siniya

The name of this classic Sephardi dish simply means fish and tahini sauce. In this version, the fish is first wrapped in vine leaves, then spread with tahini and baked. A final sprinkling of pomegranate seeds adds a fresh, invigorating flavour.

SERVES 4

4 small fish, such as trout, sea bream or
   red mullet, each weighing about
   300g/11oz, cleaned
at least 5 garlic cloves, chopped
juice of 2 lemons
75ml/5 tbsp olive oil
about 20 brined vine leaves
tahini, for drizzling
1–2 pomegranates
fresh mint and coriander (cilantro) sprigs,
   to garnish

1 Preheat the oven to 180°C/350°F/Gas 4. Put the fish in a shallow, ovenproof dish, large enough to fit the whole fish without touching each other. In a bowl, combine the garlic, lemon juice and oil, and spoon over the fish. Turn the fish to coat.

2 Rinse the vine leaves well under cold water, then wrap the fish in the leaves. Arrange the fish in the same dish and spoon any marinade in the dish over the top of each. Bake for 30 minutes.

3 Drizzle the tahini over the top of each wrapped fish, making a ribbon so that the tops and tails of the fish and some of the vine leaf wrapping still show. Return to the oven and bake for a further 5–10 minutes, or until the top is golden and slightly crusted.

4 Meanwhile, cut the pomegranates in half and carefully scoop out the seeds with a teaspoon. Sprinkle the seeds over the fish, garnish with mint and coriander sprigs, and serve immediately.

Nutritional information per portion: Energy 402kcal/1681kJ; Protein 46.8g; Carbohydrate 2.6g, of which sugars 2.6g; Fat 22.8g, of which saturates 4.1g; Cholesterol 192mg; Calcium 86mg; Fibre 0.5g; Sodium 176mg.

Dag ha sfarim

A whole fish, cooked in spices, is a festival treat. It is especially popular at Rosh Hashanah, when the Sephardi community eat whole fish. The wholeness symbolizes the full year to come and the head symbolizes the wisdom that we ask to be endowed with.

SERVES 6–8

1–1.5kg/2¼–3¼lb snapper, cleaned,
   with head and tail left on (optional)
2.5ml/½ tsp salt
juice of 2 lemons
45–60ml/3–4 tbsp extra virgin olive oil
2 onions, sliced
5 garlic cloves, chopped
1 green (bell) pepper, chopped
1–2 fresh green chillies, finely chopped
2.5ml/½ tsp ground turmeric
2.5ml/½ tsp curry powder
2.5 ml/½ tsp ground cumin
120ml/4fl oz/½ cup passata
   (bottled strained tomatoes)
5–6 canned tomatoes, chopped
45–60ml/3–4 tbsp chopped fresh parsley
   leaves, plus extra to garnish
65g/2½oz pine nuts, toasted

1 Prick the fish all over with a fork and rub with the salt. Put the fish in a non-metallic roasting pan or dish and pour over the lemon juice. Leave to stand for 2 hours.

2 Preheat the oven to 180°C/ 350°F/Gas 4. Heat the oil in a pan, add the onions and half the garlic and fry for about 5 minutes, or until softened.

3 Add the pepper, chillies, turmeric, curry powder and cumin to the pan and cook gently for 2–3 minutes.

4 Stir the passata, tomatoes and chopped parsley into the pan.

5 Sprinkle half of the pine nuts over the base of a large ovenproof dish, top with half of the sauce, then add the fish and its marinade.

6 Sprinkle the remaining garlic over the fish, then add the remaining sauce and the remaining pine nuts. Cover tightly with a lid or foil and bake in the oven for about 30 minutes, or until the fish is tender. Garnish with parsley and serve.

Nutritional information per portion: Energy 195kcal/815kJ; Protein 14.3g; Carbohydrate 6.7g, of which sugars 5.8g; Fat 12.6g, of which saturates 1g; Cholesterol 0mg; Calcium 62mg; Fibre 1.6g; Sodium 104mg.

Meat and poultry

To the Ashkenazim, meat was the most important of foods, but for the Jews of the shtetl, eating meat tended to be little more than a smear of chicken fat on a piece of rye bread. Classic Ashkenazi meat dishes are rich with robust flavours: meats braised with onions and eaten with kasha, and beef stewed into a cholent.

Kofta kebabs

These spicy patties of minced lamb are spiked with aromatic herbs and seasonings. They are very popular in both Jewish communities and non-Jewish communities from the Middle East.

SERVES 4

450g/1lb minced (ground) lamb
1–2 large slices of French bread, crumbled
1/2 bunch coriander (cilantro), chopped
5 garlic cloves, chopped
1 onion, finely chopped
juice of 1/2 lemon
5ml/1 tsp ground cumin
5ml/1 tsp paprika
15ml/1 tbsp curry powder
pinch each of ground cardamom, turmeric
     and cinnamon
cayenne pepper or chopped fresh
     chillies (optional)
15ml/1 tbsp tomato purée (paste)
1 egg, beaten, if needed
salt and ground black pepper
flatbread and salads, to serve

1 Put the lamb, crumbled bread, coriander, garlic, onion, lemon juice, spices, tomato purée, cayenne pepper or chillies, if using, and seasoning in a large bowl. Mix well. If the mixture does not bind together, add the beaten egg and a little more bread.

2 With wet hands, shape the mixture into four large or eight small patties.

3 Heat a heavy non-stick frying pan, add the patties and cook, taking care that they do not fall apart, turning once or twice, until browned. Serve hot with flatbread and salads.

Nutritional information per portion: Energy 280kcal/1173kJ; Protein 23.9g; Carbohydrate 12.1g, of which sugars 1.4g; Fat 15.5g, of which saturates 7.1g; Cholesterol 87mg; Calcium 70mg; Fibre 1.2g; Sodium 214mg.

Jerusalem barbecued lamb kebabs

In the early days of the modern state of Israel, "lamb" kebabs would have been made with turkey and a little lamb fat. Turkey, chicken, beef and veal can all be cooked in this way.

SERVES 4–6

800g/1¾lb tender lamb, cubed
1.5ml/¼ tsp ground allspice
1.5ml/¼ tsp ground cinnamon
1.5ml/¼ tsp ground black pepper
1.5ml/¼ tsp ground cardamom
45–60ml/3–4 tbsp chopped
    fresh parsley
2 onions, chopped
5–8 garlic cloves, chopped
juice of ½ lemon
45ml/3 tbsp extra virgin olive oil
sumac, for sprinkling (optional)
30ml/2 tbsp pine nuts
salt
flatbreads, tahini and mixed salad,
    to serve

1 Mix the lamb, allspice, cinnamon, black pepper, cardamom, half the parsley, half the onions, the garlic, lemon juice and olive oil together. Season with salt now or sprinkle on after cooking. Leave to marinate.

2 Meanwhile, light the barbecue and leave for 40 minutes. When the coals are white and grey, the barbecue is ready for cooking. If using wooden skewers, soak them in water for 30 minutes to prevent them from burning.

3 Thread the cubes of meat on to presoaked wooden or metal skewers, then cook for 2–3 minutes on each side until cooked and browned.

4 Transfer the kebabs to a serving dish and sprinkle with the reserved onions, parsley, sumac, if using, pine nuts and salt, if you like. Serve with flatbreads, tahini and a mixed salad.

Nutritional information per portion: Energy 514kcal/2138kJ; Protein 41.4g; Carbohydrate 6.4g, of which sugars 4.7g; Fat 36.1g, of which saturates 11.9g; Cholesterol 152mg; Calcium 51mg; Fibre 1.6g; Sodium 177mg.

Lamb with globe artichokes

In this Italian Jewish dish, a garlic-studded leg of lamb is cooked with red wine and artichoke hearts, making it not only elegant but a dish worthy of any special feast or gathering.

SERVES 6–8

1 kosher leg of lamb, about 2kg/4¹/₂lb
1–2 garlic heads, divided into cloves,
    peeled and thinly sliced, leaving
    5–6 peeled but whole
handful of fresh rosemary, stalks
    removed (about 25g/1oz)
500ml/17fl oz/2¹/₄ cups dry red wine

30ml/2 tbsp olive oil
4 globe artichokes
1 tsp lemon juice
5 shallots, chopped
250ml/8fl oz/1 cup beef stock
salt and ground black pepper
green salad with garlic croûtons, to serve

1 With a sharp knife, make incisions all over the lamb. Into each incision, put a sliver of garlic and as many rosemary leaves as you can. Season with salt and black pepper. Place in a non-metallic dish and pour the olive oil and half the wine and over the top. Leave to marinate until you are ready to roast it.

2 Preheat the oven to 230°C/450°F/Gas 8. Put the meat and the marinade in a roasting pan and surround with the whole garlic cloves. Roast for 15 minutes, then reduce to 160°C/325°F/Gas 3 and cook for a further 1 hour, or until the lamb is cooked to your liking.

3 Meanwhile, prepare the artichokes. Pull back their leaves and let them snap off. Trim the rough ends off the base. Cut into quarters and cut out the inside thistle heart. Place the quarters into a bowl of water to which you have added the lemon juice, to prevent discolouring. About 20 minutes before the lamb is cooked, drain the artichokes and place around the meat. When the lamb is cooked, transfer the meat and artichokes to a serving dish. Carefully pour the meat juices and roasted garlic into a pan.

4 Spoon off the fat from the juices and add the chopped shallots and the remaining red wine. Cook over a high heat until the liquid has reduced to a very small amount, then add the beef stock and cook, stirring constantly, until the juices are flavourful. Coat the lamb and artichokes with the roasted garlic and red wine sauce and garnish with rosemary. Serve with green salad and garlic croûtons.

COOK'S TIP
If you do not have access to a kosher leg of lamb with the sciatic nerve removed, you can use lamb riblets or shoulder of lamb instead.

Nutritional information per portion: Energy 595kcal/2487kJ; Protein 72.4g; Carbohydrate 2.2g, of which sugars 1.6g; Fat 28.3g, of which saturates 11.4g; Cholesterol 275mg; Calcium 53mg; Fibre 0.5g; Sodium 217mg.

Moroccan lamb with honey and prunes

This dish is eaten by Moroccan Jews at Rosh Hashanah, when sweet foods are traditionally served in anticipation of a sweet New Year to come.

SERVES 6

130g/4¹/₂oz/¹/₂ cup pitted prunes
350ml/12fl oz/1¹/₂ cups hot tea
1kg/2¹/₄lb stewing or braising lamb
115g/4oz/1 cup blanched almonds
1 onion, chopped
75–90ml/5–6 tbsp chopped fresh parsley
2.5ml/¹/₂ tsp ground ginger
2.5ml/¹/₂ tsp curry powder
pinch of freshly grated nutmeg
10ml/2 tsp ground cinnamon
1.5ml/¹/₄ tsp saffron threads
30ml/2 tbsp hot water
75–120ml/5–9 tbsp honey, to taste
250ml/8fl oz/1 cup beef or lamb stock
30ml/2 tbsp chopped coriander (cilantro)
3 hard-boiled eggs, cut into wedges
salt and ground black pepper

1 Preheat the oven to 180°C/ 350°F/Gas 4. Soak the prunes in the tea until they plump up. Meanwhile, cut the lamb into chunks and toast the almonds.

2 Put the lamb, chopped onion, parsley, ginger, curry powder, nutmeg, cinnamon, salt and a large pinch of ground black pepper in a roasting pan. Cover and cook in the oven for about 2 hours, or until the meat is tender.

3 Drain the prunes; add their liquid to the lamb. Combine the saffron and hot water and add to the pan with the honey and stock. Bake, uncovered, for 30 minutes, turning the lamb occasionally.

4 Add the plumped prunes to the pan and stir gently to mix. Serve immediately sprinkled with the toasted almonds and chopped coriander, and topped with the wedges of hard-boiled egg.

Nutritional information per portion: Energy 618kcal/2564kJ; Protein 42.7g; Carbohydrate 0.8g, of which sugars 0.1g; Fat 49.3g, of which saturates 21.2g; Cholesterol 183mg; Calcium 16mg; Fibre 0.2g; Sodium 150mg.

Lamb pot-roasted with tomato sauce, beans and onions

This slow-braised dish of lamb with beans, stewed in a spicy tomato sauce, shows a Greek influence. It is also good made with courgettes instead of beans.

SERVES 8

8 garlic cloves, chopped
2.5–5ml/¹/₂–1 tsp ground cumin
45ml/3 tbsp olive oil
juice of 1 lemon
1kg/2¹/₄lb lamb on the bone
2 onions, thinly sliced
500ml/17fl oz/2¹/₄ cups lamb stock
75–90ml/5–6 tbsp tomato purée (paste)
1 cinnamon stick
2–3 large pinches of ground allspice
15–30ml/1–2 tbsp sugar, to taste
400g/14oz/3 cups runner (green)
   beans, sliced
salt and ground black pepper
15–30ml/1–2 tbsp chopped
   fresh parsley, to garnish

1 Preheat the oven to 160°C/325°F/Gas 3. In a bowl, mix the garlic, cumin, olive oil, lemon juice, salt and pepper, add the lamb and toss to coat.

2 Heat a flameproof casserole and sear the lamb on all sides. Add the onions and pour the stock over the meat to cover. Stir in the tomato purée, spices and sugar. Cover and cook for 2–3 hours, depending how well done you like it.

3 Remove the casserole from the oven and pour the stock into a pan. Move the onions to the side of the dish and return to the oven, uncovered, for 20 minutes.

4 Meanwhile, add the beans to the stock and cook until the beans are tender and the sauce has thickened.

5 Slice the meat and serve with the pan juices and beans, garnished with parsley.

Nutritional information per portion: Energy 371kcal/1544kJ; Protein 26.3g; Carbohydrate 7.9g, of which sugars 6.5g; Fat 26.4g, of which saturates 10.9g; Cholesterol 104mg; Calcium 40mg; Fibre 1.9g; Sodium 103mg.

Pot-roasted brisket

This big, pot-roasted meat dish includes the traditional kishke, a heavy, sausage-shaped dumpling, which is added to the pot and cooked with the meat. Serve with kasha varnishkes – meat gravy with kasha is one of life's perfect combinations.

SERVES 6–8

5 onions, sliced

3 bay leaves

1–1.6kg/2¼–3½lb beef brisket

1 garlic head, broken into cloves

4 carrots, thickly sliced

10ml/2 tsp paprika

500ml/17fl oz/2¼ cups beef stock

3–4 baking potatoes, peeled and quartered

salt and ground black pepper

FOR THE KISHKE

250g/9oz/2¼ cups plain
  (all-purpose) flour

120ml/4fl oz/½ cup semolina

15ml/1 tbsp paprika

1 carrot, grated, and 2 carrots,
  diced (optional)

250ml/8fl oz/1 cup rendered
  chicken fat

30ml/2 tbsp crisp, fried onions

½ onion, grated, and 3 onions,
  thinly sliced

3 garlic cloves, chopped

salt and ground black pepper

90cm/36in sausage casing

1 Preheat the oven to 180°C/350°F/Gas 4. Put one-third of the onions and a bay leaf in an ovenproof dish, then top with the brisket. Sprinkle over the garlic, carrots and remaining bay leaves and season. Top with the remaining onions. Pour stock to a depth of 5–7.5cm/2–3in and cover with foil. Cook in the oven for 2 hours.

2 Meanwhile, make the kishke. Combine all the ingredients and stuff the mixture into the casing, leaving enough space for the mixture to expand. Tie into sausage-shaped lengths.

3 When the meat has cooked for 2 hours, add the kishke and potatoes, re-cover and cook for a further 1 hour until the meat and potatoes are tender.

4 Remove the foil and increase the temperature to 190°C/375°F/Gas 5. Move the onions away from the top of the meat and return to the oven for a further 30 minutes. Serve hot or cold.

Nutritional information per portion: Energy 781kcal/3271kJ; Protein 44.2g; Carbohydrate 74g, of which sugars 12.7g; Fat 36.4g, of which saturates 14.4g; Cholesterol 113mg; Calcium 124mg; Fibre 5g; Sodium 124mg.

Holishkes

These stuffed cabbage leaves are a traditional dish for Sukkot, the harvest festival in autumn. Versions of this dish have been enjoyed by Jewish communities in the Middle East and Europe.

SERVES 6–8

1kg/2¼lb lean minced (ground) beef
75g/3oz/scant ½ cup long grain rice
4 onions, 2 chopped and 2 sliced
5–8 garlic cloves, chopped
2 eggs
45ml/3 tbsp water
1 large head of white or
    green cabbage
400g/14oz can chopped tomatoes
45ml/3 tbsp demerara (raw) sugar
45ml/3 tbsp white wine vinegar,
    cider vinegar or lemon juice
pinch of ground cinnamon
salt and ground black pepper
lemon wedges, to serve

1 Put the beef, rice, 5ml/1 tsp salt, pepper, chopped onions and garlic in a bowl. Beat the eggs with the water, and combine with the meat mixture. Chill.

2 Cut the core from the cabbage in a cone shape and discard. Bring a large pan of water to the boil and blanch the cabbage for 1 minute, then remove from the pan. Peel one or two layers of leaves off the head, then replace it in the hot water. Repeat until all the leaves are removed.

3 Preheat the oven to 150°C/300°F/Gas 2. Form the beef mixture into ovals and wrap each in one or two cabbage leaves.

4 Lay the rolls in an ovenproof dish, alternating with the sliced onions. Pour the tomatoes over and add the sugar, vinegar, seasoning and cinnamon. Cover and bake for 2 hours, basting with the tomato juices, then uncover and cook for 30–60 minutes until the sauce is thickened. Serve with lemon wedges.

Nutritional information per portion: Energy 425kcal/1773kJ; Protein 29.7g; Carbohydrate 27.5g, of which sugars 17.6g; Fat 22.3g, of which saturates 9.2g; Cholesterol 123mg; Calcium 86mg; Fibre 3.7g; Sodium 134mg.

Bachi's braised minced beef patties with onions

This is one of the dishes my New Yorker grandmother used to make. She often added extra vegetables with the onions, such as sliced green peppers, broccoli or mushrooms.

SERVES 4

500g/1¼lb lean minced
   (ground) beef
4–6 garlic cloves, coarsely chopped
4 onions, 1 finely chopped and
   3 sliced
15–30ml/1–2 tbsp soy sauce
15–30ml/1–2 tbsp vegetable oil
   (optional)
2–3 green (bell) peppers, sliced
   lengthways into strips
ground black pepper
salad, to serve

1 Place the minced beef, garlic and chopped onions in a bowl and mix well. Season with soy sauce and pepper and form into four large or eight small patties.

2 Heat a non-stick pan, add a little oil, if you like, then add the patties and cook until browned. Splash over soy sauce.

3 Cover the patties with the sliced onions and peppers, add a little soy sauce, then cover the pan. Reduce the heat to very low, and braise for 20–30 minutes.

4 When the onions are turning golden brown, remove the pan from the heat. Serve the patties, with the onions and salad.

Nutritional information per portion: Energy 347kcal/1442kJ; Protein 26.8g; Carbohydrate 13.8g, of which sugars 11.2g; Fat 20.8g, of which saturates 8.8g; Cholesterol 75mg; Calcium 44mg; Fibre 2.8g; Sodium 374mg.

Roasted chicken with grapes and fresh root ginger

This dish, with its blend of spices and sweet fruit, is inspired by Moroccan flavours. Serve with couscous, mixed with a handful of cooked chickpeas.

SERVES 4

1–1.6kg/2¼–3½lb chicken
115–130g/4–4½oz fresh root
    ginger, grated
6–8 garlic cloves, roughly chopped
juice of 1 lemon
about 30ml/2 tbsp olive oil
2–3 large pinches of ground cinnamon

500g/1¼lb seeded red and
    green grapes
500g/1¼lb seedless green grapes
5–7 shallots, chopped
about 250ml/8fl oz/1 cup chicken or
    vegetable stock
salt and ground black pepper

1 Rub the chicken with half of the ginger, the garlic, half of the lemon juice, the olive oil, cinnamon, salt and lots of pepper. Leave to marinate. Meanwhile, cut the red and green seeded grapes in half, remove the seeds and set aside. Add the whole green seedless grapes to the halved ones.

2 Preheat the oven to 180°C/350°F/Gas 4. Heat a flameproof casserole until hot. Remove the chicken from the marinade, add to the casserole and cook until browned on all sides. (There should be enough oil on the chicken to brown it but, if not, add a little extra.)

3 Put some of the shallots into the chicken cavity with the garlic and ginger from the marinade and as many of the grapes as will fit inside. Roast for 40 minutes, or until the chicken is cooked through.

4 Remove the chicken from the pan and keep warm. Pour off any oil from the pan, reserving any sediment in the base. Add the remaining shallots to the pan and cook for 5 minutes until softened.

5 Add half the remaining red and green grapes, the remaining ginger, the stock and any juices from the roast chicken and cook over a medium-high heat until the grapes have cooked down to a thick sauce. Season with salt, ground black pepper and the remaining lemon juice to taste.

6 Serve the chicken on a warmed serving dish, surrounded by the sauce and the reserved grapes.

Nutritional information per portion: Energy 454kcal/1891kJ; Protein 31.6g; Carbohydrate 19.5g, of which sugars 19.5g; Fat 28.1g, of which saturates 7.1g; Cholesterol 165mg; Calcium 28mg; Fibre 1g; Sodium 116mg.

Sephardi spiced chicken rice with **lemon** and **mint relish**

This is a lighter, quicker version of hameen, the long-simmered Shabbat stew. This modern version is more refreshing than the heavier original.

SERVES 4

250g/9oz chicken, skinned and diced
3 garlic cloves, chopped
5ml/1 tsp ground turmeric
30ml/2 tbsp olive oil
2 small to medium carrots, diced or
   chopped
seeds from 6–8 cardamom pods
500g/1¼lb/2½ cups long grain rice
250g/9oz tomatoes, chopped
750ml/1¼ pints/3 cups chicken stock

FOR THE RELISH
3 tomatoes, diced
1 bunch or large handful of fresh mint,
   chopped
5–8 spring onions (scallions),
   thinly sliced
juice of 2 lemons
salt

1 To make the relish, put all the ingredients in a bowl and mix together. Chill until ready to serve.

2 Mix the diced chicken with half the garlic and the turmeric. Heat a little of the oil in a pan, add the chicken and fry briefly until the chicken has changed colour and is almost cooked. Remove from the pan and set aside.

3 Add the carrots to the pan with the remaining oil, then stir in the remaining garlic, cardamom seeds and the rice. Cook for 1 minute.

4 Add the tomatoes and chicken stock to the pan and bring to the boil. Cover and simmer for about 10 minutes, until the rice is tender. A few minutes before the rice is cooked, fork in the chicken. Serve with the relish.

Nutritional information per portion: Energy 633kcal/2648kJ, Protein 26.1g, Carbohydrate 107.7g, of which sugars 7.7g; Fat 10.3g, of which saturates 1.6g; Cholesterol 44mg; Calcium 76mg; Fibre 3.1g; Sodium 64mg.

Turkey or chicken schnitzel

Schnitzel is a pounded-flat, crisp-coated, fried steak of turkey, chicken or veal. In the old country of Austria, schnitzel was made from veal. Today in Israel it is usually made of turkey and is immensely popular. Serve with a selection of vegetables.

SERVES 4

4 boneless turkey or chicken breast
    fillets, each weighing about 175g/6oz
juice of 1 lemon
2 garlic cloves, chopped
plain (all-purpose) flour, for dusting
1–2 eggs
15ml/1 tbsp water
about 50g/2oz/¹/₂ cup matzo meal
paprika
a mixture of vegetable and olive oil, for
    shallow frying
salt and ground black pepper
lemon wedges and a selection of
    vegetables, to serve (optional)

1 Lay each piece of meat between two sheets of greaseproof (waxed) paper and pound with a mallet until it is about half its original thickness and even. Combine the lemon juice, garlic, salt and pepper. Coat the meat in the mixture, then leave to marinate.

2 Meanwhile, arrange three wide plates or shallow dishes in a row. Fill one plate or dish with flour, beat the egg and water together in another, and mix the matzo meal, salt, pepper and paprika together on the third.

3 Dip each fillet into the flour, then the egg, then the matzo. Pat everything in well, then chill for at least 30 minutes, and up to 2 hours.

4 In a large frying pan, heat the oil until turns a cube of bread golden brown in 30–60 seconds. Add the fillets, in batches, and fry until golden brown, turning once. Drain and serve with lemon wedges and vegetables.

Nutritional information per portion: Energy 368kcal/1546kJ; Protein 45.4g; Carbohydrate 14.7g, of which sugars 0.6g; Fat 14.6g, of which saturates 2.3g; Cholesterol 170mg; Calcium 27mg; Fibre 0.5g; Sodium 125mg.

Doro wat

Long-simmered Ethiopian stews, known as wats, are often made for Shabbat. They are traditionally served with the pancake-like flatbread, injera, which is made before the Sabbath and wrapped in a clean cloth until the wat is ready to eat.

SERVES 4

90ml/6 tbsp vegetable oil
6–8 onions, chopped
6 garlic cloves, chopped
10ml/2 tsp chopped fresh root ginger
400g/14oz can chopped tomatoes
1.3kg/3lb chicken, cut into 8–12 pieces
seeds from 5–8 cardamom pods
2.5ml/1/2 tsp ground turmeric
large pinch of ground cinnamon
large pinch of ground cloves
large pinch of grated nutmeg
cayenne pepper, to taste
4 hard-boiled eggs
fresh coriander (cilantro) and
    onion rings, to garnish
injera, flatbread or rice, to serve

1 Heat the oil in a pan, add the onions and cook for 10 minutes until softened. Add the garlic and ginger and cook for 1–2 minutes.

2 Add 250ml/8fl oz/1 cup water and the tomatoes. Bring to the boil and cook, stirring, for 10 minutes, until the liquid has reduced and the mixture has thickened. Season with salt and ground black pepper.

3 Add the chicken and spices to the pan and turn the chicken in the sauce. Lower the heat, then cover and simmer for 1 hour, or until the chicken is cooked through. Add a little more water if the mixture seems too thick.

4 Shell the eggs and prick them once or twice with a fork. Add the eggs to the sauce and heat gently until the eggs are warmed through. Garnish with coriander and onion rings and serve with injera, flatbread or rice.

Nutritional information per portion: Energy 764kcal/3169kJ; Protein 48.8g; Carbohydrate 17.7g, of which sugars 13.1g; Fat 55.9g, of which saturates 13.2g; Cholesterol 398mg; Calcium 101mg; Fibre 3.2g; Sodium 382mg.

Petti di pollo all'ebraica

This Italian dish strongly reflects the traditions of both Mediterranean and Jewish cooking. Jews favour the enrichment of meat sauces with egg because of the laws of the Kashrut, which forbids the addition of cream to meat dishes.

SERVES 4

4 skinless, boneless chicken
   breast portions
plain (all-purpose) flour, for dusting
30–45ml/2–3 tbsp olive oil
1–2 onions, chopped
¼ fennel bulb, chopped (optional)
15ml/1 tbsp chopped fresh parsley, plus
   extra to garnish

7.5ml/1½ tsp fennel seeds
75ml/5 tbsp dry Marsala
120ml/4fl oz/½ cup chicken stock
300g/11oz/2¼ cups petits pois
   (baby peas)
juice of 1½ lemons
2 egg yolks
salt and ground black pepper

1 Season the chicken with salt and pepper, then dust generously with flour. Shake off the excess flour and set aside.

2 Heat half the oil in a pan, add the onions, fennel, if using, parsley and fennel seeds. Cook for 5 minutes. Add the remaining oil and the chicken and cook for 2–3 minutes on each side, until lightly browned. Remove the chicken and onion mixture from the pan and set aside.

3 Deglaze the pan by pouring in the Marsala and cooking over a high heat until reduced to about 30ml/2 tbsp, then pour in the stock. Add the peas and return the chicken and onion mixture to the pan. Cook over a very low heat while you prepare the egg mixture.

4 In a bowl, beat the lemon juice and egg yolks together, then slowly add about 120ml/4fl oz/½ cup of the hot liquid from the chicken and peas, stirring well to combine.

5 Return the mixture to the pan and cook over a low heat, stirring, until the mixture thickens slightly. (Do not allow the mixture to boil or the eggs will curdle and spoil the sauce.) Serve the chicken immediately, sprinkled with a little extra chopped fresh parsley.

Nutritional information per portion: Energy 375kcal/1567kJ; Protein 43.4g; Carbohydrate 14.9g, of which sugars 7g; Fat 13.9g, of which saturates 2.6g; Cholesterol 206mg; Calcium 51mg; Fibre 4.5g; Sodium 99mg.

Mild green Calcutta curry of chicken and vegetables

The addition of coconut milk creates a rich sauce that is sweet with dried and fresh fruit and fragrant with herbs. It is perfect for those keeping Kashrut as it has a creamy character yet contains no dairy products. Serve with hot naan or steamed rice.

SERVES 4

4 garlic cloves, chopped

15ml/1 tbsp chopped fresh root ginger

2–3 chillies, chopped

1/2 bunch fresh coriander (cilantro) leaves, roughly chopped

1 onion, chopped

juice of 1 lemon

pinch of cayenne pepper

2.5ml/1/2 tsp curry powder

2.5ml/1/2 tsp ground cumin

2–3 pinches of ground cloves

large pinch of ground coriander

3 boneless chicken breast portions or thighs, skinned and cut into bitesize pieces

30ml/2 tbsp vegetable oil

2 cinnamon sticks

250ml/8fl oz/1 cup chicken stock

250ml/8fl oz/1 cup coconut milk

15–30ml/1–2 tbsp sugar, to taste

1–2 bananas

1/4 pineapple, peeled and chopped

handful of sultanas (golden raisins)

handful of raisins or currants

2–3 sprigs of fresh mint, thinly sliced

juice of 1/4–1/2 lemon, to taste

salt

1 Purée the garlic, ginger, chillies, fresh coriander, onion, lemon juice, cayenne pepper, curry powder, cumin, cloves, ground coriander and salt in a food processor or blender. Toss together the chicken pieces with 30ml/2 tbsp of the spice mixture and set aside.

2 Heat the oil in a wok or large frying pan, then add the remaining spice mixture and cook over a medium heat, stirring, for about 10 minutes, or until the paste is lightly browned. Stir the cinnamon sticks, stock, coconut milk and sugar into the pan, bring to the boil, then reduce the heat and simmer for 10 minutes. Then add the chicken to the sauce and cook for 2 minutes, or until the chicken becomes opaque.

3 Meanwhile, thickly slice the bananas. Stir all the fruit into the curry and cook for 1–2 minutes. Stir in the mint and lemon juice. Check the seasoning and add more salt, spice and lemon juice if necessary.

Nutritional information per portion: Energy 383kcal/1622kJ; Protein 29.5g; Carbohydrate 52.8g, of which sugars 51.5g; Fat 7.5g, of which saturates 1.2g; Cholesterol 79mg; Calcium 92mg; Fibre 2.6g; Sodium 150mg.

Israeli barbecued chicken

Barbecued chicken is ubiquitous in Israel and it seems that every street corner kiosk and stall sells a version of this aromatic treat. In this recipe, the Egyptian-inspired marinade is strongly scented with cumin and cinnamon.

SERVES 4

5 garlic cloves, chopped

30ml/2 tbsp ground cumin

7.5ml/1½ tsp ground cinnamon

5ml/1 tsp paprika

juice of 1 lemon

30ml/2 tbsp olive oil

1.3kg/3lb chicken, cut into 8 portions

salt and ground black pepper

fresh coriander (cilantro) leaves,
   to garnish

warmed pitta bread, salad and
   lemon wedges, to serve

1 In a bowl, combine the garlic, cumin, cinnamon, paprika, lemon juice, oil, salt and pepper. Add the chicken and turn to coat thoroughly. Leave to marinate for at least 1 hour or cover and place in the refrigerator overnight.

2 Light the barbecue. After about 40 minutes it will be ready for cooking.

3 Arrange the dark meat on the grill (broiler) and cook for 10 minutes, turning once.

4 Grill (broil) the remaining chicken for 7–10 minutes, turning occasionally, until golden brown and the juices run clear when pricked with a skewer. Serve immediately, with pitta breads, lemon wedges and salad.

Nutritional information per portion: Energy 481kcal/1997kJ; Protein 40.8g; Carbohydrate 1g, of which sugars 0.1g; Fat 34.8g, of which saturates 8.9g; Cholesterol 215mg; Calcium 14mg; Fibre 0.3g; Sodium 147mg.

Vegetable dishes and salads

The repertoire of Jewish vegetable dishes is wide and varied, no doubt partly because when kosher meat or cooking equipment is not available, a vegetarian meal is often the only option. Vegetable cutlets and schnitzel are popular Israeli dishes, as are the many zesty vegetable stews, while the Sephardi kitchen boasts a long tradition of vegetable salads.

Split pea or lentil fritters

These simple fritters are very quick and easy to make. You can use a chopped fresh green chilli instead of the cayenne pepper, if you like. Serve them hot or at room temperature.

SERVES 4–6

250g/9oz/generous 1 cup yellow split
    peas or red lentils, soaked overnight
3–5 garlic cloves, chopped
30ml/2 tbsp chopped fresh root ginger
120ml/4fl oz/¹/₂ cup chopped fresh
    coriander (cilantro) leaves
2.5–5ml/¹/₂–1 tsp ground cumin
1.5–2.5ml/¹/₄–¹/₂ tsp ground turmeric
large pinch of cayenne pepper
50g/2oz/¹/₂ cup gram (besan) flour
5ml/1 tsp baking powder
30ml/2 tbsp couscous
2 large or 3 small onions, chopped
vegetable oil, for frying
salt and ground black pepper
salad and lemon wedges, to serve

1 Drain the split peas or lentils, reserving a little of the soaking water. Mince (grind) the garlic and ginger in a food processor. Add the split peas, 15–30ml/1–2 tbsp of the reserved water and the coriander, and process to a purée.

2 Add the cumin, turmeric, cayenne, 2.5ml/¹/₂ tsp salt, 2.5ml/¹/₂ tsp pepper, the flour, baking powder and couscous and combine to a thick batter. If too thick, add a spoonful of soaking water and if too watery, add a little more flour. Mix in the onions.

3 Heat the oil in a wide, deep frying pan, to a depth of 5cm/2in, until it is hot enough to brown a cube of bread in 30 seconds. Using two spoons, form the mixture into two-bitesize balls and slip each one into the hot oil. Cook until golden brown, then turn and cook the second side until golden brown.

4 Remove the fritters with a slotted spoon and drain on kitchen paper. Keep the fritters warm in the oven until all the mixture is cooked. Serve with salad and lemon wedges.

Nutritional information per portion: Energy 360kcal/1511kJ; Protein 14.1g; Carbohydrate 51.3g, of which sugars 8.3g; Fat 12.3g, of which saturates 1.4g; Cholesterol 0mg; Calcium 119mg; Fibre 5.3g; Sodium 26mg.

Falafel

The secret to good falafel is using well-soaked, but not cooked, chickpeas. Do not use canned chickpeas as the texture will be mushy and the falafel will fall apart when they are fried.

SERVES 6

250g/9oz/1⅓ cups dried chickpeas
1 litre/1¾ pints/4 cups water
45–60ml/3–4 tbsp bulgur wheat
1 large or 2 small onions, finely chopped
5 garlic cloves, crushed
75ml/5 tbsp chopped fresh parsley
75ml/5 tbsp chopped fresh coriander
    (cilantro) leaves
45ml/3 tbsp ground cumin
15ml/1 tbsp ground coriander
5ml/1 tsp baking powder
5m/1 tsp salt
small pinch ground black pepper
small pinch cayenne pepper
5ml/1 tsp curry powder (optional)
45–60ml/3–4 tbsp gram (besan) flour
vegetable oil, for deep-frying

1 Put the chickpeas in a large bowl. Pour in the water and leave to soak for at least 4 hours, then drain and mince (grind) in a food processor.

2 Put the minced chickpeas in a bowl and stir in the bulgur wheat, onion, garlic, parsley, fresh coriander, ground cumin and coriander, baking powder, salt, pepper, cayenne pepper, and curry powder, if using.

3 Stir in 45ml/3 tbsp water and leave for 45 minutes.

4 Stir the gram flour into the batter, adding a little water if it is too thick or a little wholemeal flour if too thin. Shape heaped tablespoons of the mixture into 12–18 balls.

5 Heat the oil for deep-frying until it is hot enough to brown a cube of bread in 30 seconds. Lower the heat. Cook the falafel in batches for 3–4 minutes until golden brown. Remove with a slotted spoon and drain on kitchen paper before adding more to the oil. Serve.

Nutritional information per portion: Energy 303kcal/1282kJ; Protein 18.5g; Carbohydrate 44.7g, of which sugars 5.2g; Fat 6.9g, of which saturates 1.2g; Cholesterol 0mg; Calcium 88mg; Fibre 7.2g; Sodium 16mg.

Sephardi stuffed onions, potatoes and courgettes

The vegetarian filling of these vegetables is tomato-red, Yemenite-spiced and accented with the tart taste of lemon juice. They are delicious cold and are excellent served as an appetizer as well as a main course. Serve warm with a mixed salad, if you like.

SERVES 4

4 potatoes, peeled
4 onions, skinned
4 courgettes (zucchini),
    halved widthways
2–4 garlic cloves, chopped
45–60ml/3–4 tbsp olive oil
45–60ml/3–4 tbsp tomato
    purée (paste)
1.5ml/¼ tsp ras al hanout or
    curry powder

large pinch of ground allspice
seeds of 2–3 cardamom pods
juice of ¹/₂ lemon
30–45ml/2–3 tbsp chopped
    fresh parsley
about 90–120ml/6–8 tbsp vegetable
    stock
salt and ground black pepper
salad, to serve (optional)

1 Bring a large pan of salted water to the boil. Starting with the potatoes, then the onions and finally the courgettes, add to the boiling water and cook until they become almost tender but not cooked through. Allow about 10 minutes for the potatoes, 8 minutes for the onions and 4–6 minutes for the courgettes. Remove the vegetables from the pan and leave to cool.

2 When the vegetables are cool enough to handle, hollow them out. Preheat the oven to 190°C/375°F/Gas 5.

3 Finely chop the cut-out vegetable flesh and put it in a bowl. Add the garlic, half the olive oil, the tomato purée, ras al hanout or curry powder, allspice, cardamom seeds, lemon juice, parsley, salt and pepper and mix well together. Use the stuffing mixture to fill the hollowed vegetables.

4 Arrange the stuffed vegetables in a baking tin (pan) and drizzle with the stock and the remaining oil. Roast for 35–40 minutes, or until golden brown. Serve warm with a salad, if you like.

Nutritional information per portion: Energy 347kcal/1452kJ; Protein 10.2g; Carbohydrate 56.7g, of which sugars 22.1g; Fat 10.3g, of which saturates 1.6g; Cholesterol 0mg; Calcium 135mg; Fibre 8.2g; Sodium 62mg.

Balkan aubergines with cheese

This wonderful dish is cloaked in a thick cheese sauce that, when cooked, has a topping slightly like a soufflé. It is delicious hot but even better cold, and is the perfect dish to make for a picnic.

SERVES 4–6

2 large aubergines (eggplants), cut into
    5mm/¼ in thick slices
60ml/4 tbsp olive oil
25g/1oz/2 tbsp butter
30ml/2 tbsp plain (all-purpose) flour
500ml/17fl oz/2¼ cups hot milk
about ⅛ of a nutmeg, freshly grated
4 large (US extra large) eggs,
    lightly beaten
400g/14oz/3½ cups grated cheese, such
    as kashkaval, Gruyère, or a mixture of
    Parmesan and Cheddar
cayenne pepper
salt and ground black pepper

1 Layer the aubergine slices in a colander, sprinkling each layer with salt, and leave to drain for at least 30 minutes. Rinse, then pat dry with kitchen paper.

2 Heat the oil and fry the aubergines until golden brown. Set aside.

3 Melt the butter in a pan, then add the flour and cook for I minute, stirring. Remove from the heat and gradually stir in the hot milk. Return to the heat and slowly bring to the boil, stirring, until the sauce thickens and becomes smooth. Season with nutmeg, cayenne, salt and pepper and leave to cool.

4 When the sauce is cool, beat in the eggs, then mix in the cheese, reserving a little to sprinkle on the top. Preheat the oven to 180°C/350°F/Gas 4. In an ovenproof dish, arrange a layer of the aubergines, then pour over some sauce. Repeat, ending with sauce. Sprinkle with the reserved cheese. Bake for about 35–40 minutes until golden and firm.

Nutritional information per portion: Energy 501kcal/2084kJ; Protein 25.9g; Carbohydrate 10.9g, of which sugars 6.9g; Fat 38.4g, of which saturates 19.9g; Cholesterol 206mg; Calcium 650mg; Fibre 2.2g; Sodium 599mg.

Mushroom stroganoff

This creamy sauce, studded with mushrooms, is ideal for a dinner party. Serve it with kasha, brown rice or a mixture of wild and cultivated rice.

SERVES 4

40–50g/1¹/₂–2oz/3–4 tbsp butter

500g/1¹/₄lb button (white) mushrooms, quartered

250g/9oz assorted wild or unusual mushrooms, cut into bitesize pieces

6 garlic cloves, chopped

2 onions, chopped

30ml/2 tbsp plain (all-purpose) flour

120ml/4fl oz/¹/₂ cup dry white wine

250ml/8fl oz/1 cup vegetable stock

2.5ml/¹/₂ tsp dried basil

250g/9oz crème fraîche

large pinch of freshly grated nutmeg

juice of about ¹/₄ lemon

salt and ground black pepper

chopped fresh chives, to garnish

kasha or brown or mixed rice, to serve

1 Melt a little butter in a pan and fry the mushrooms, in batches, until brown. During cooking, sprinkle the mushrooms with a little garlic, reserving half for later. Transfer the mushrooms to a plate after cooking each batch.

2 Heat the remaining butter in the pan, add the onions and fry for 5 minutes until softened. Add the remaining garlic and cook for a further 1–2 minutes, then sprinkle over the flour and cook for 1 minute, stirring constantly.

3 Remove from the heat and gradually stir in the wine and half the stock. Return to the heat and bring to the boil, stirring, until the sauce thickens and becomes smooth. Gradually stir in the remaining stock and cook until thick.

4 Add the basil and mushrooms, including their juices, to the pan. Put the crème fraîche in a bowl and stir in a little sauce, then stir the mixture into the sauce. Season with nutmeg, lemon juice, salt and pepper. Serve hot, garnished with chives and accompanied by kasha or rice.

Nutritional information per portion: Energy 408kcal/1685kJ; Protein 6.5g; Carbohydrate 14.3g, of which sugars 6.3g; Fat 34.4g, of which saturates 22.4g; Cholesterol 92mg; Calcium 81mg; Fibre 3.4g; Sodium 88mg.

Stuffed vine leaves with cumin, lemon and herbs

The important ingredients in these stuffed vine leaves are the flavourings and fresh herbs that give the brown rice filling its zest and special taste.

SERVES 6–8

250g/9oz/1¼ cups brown rice
30ml/2 tbsp natural (plain) yogurt
3 garlic cloves, chopped
1 egg, lightly beaten
5–10ml/1–2 tsp ground cumin
2.5ml/½ tsp ground cinnamon
several handfuls of raisins
3–4 spring onions (scallions), thinly sliced
½ bunch fresh mint, chopped, plus extra
   to garnish
25 preserved or fresh vine leaves
salt, if necessary

FOR COOKING
8–10 unpeeled garlic cloves
juice of 1 lemon
90ml/6 tbsp olive oil

FOR SERVING
1 lemon, cut into wedges or half slices
15–25 Greek black olives
150ml/¼ pint/⅔ cup natural
   (plain) yogurt
5ml/1 tsp paprika

1 Put the rice in a pan with 300ml/½ pint/1¼ cups water. Bring to the boil, lower the heat, cover and simmer for 30 minutes until tender. Drain and leave to cool slightly, then combine the rice with the yogurt, garlic, egg, ground cumin and cinnamon, raisins, spring onions and mint.

2 If using preserved vine leaves, rinse well. If using fresh, blanch in salted boiling water for 2–3 minutes, then rinse and drain. Lay the leaves on a board, shiny side down. Place 15–30ml/1–2 tbsp of the mixture near the stalk of each leaf. Fold each one up, starting at the bottom, then the sides, and finally rolling up towards the top to enclose the filling.

3 Layer the rolls in a steamer and stud with the garlic cloves. Fill the base of the steamer with water and drizzle the lemon juice and oil over the rolls. Cover and cook over a medium-high heat for 40 minutes, adding more water if necessary. Set the vine leaves aside to cool slightly. Garnish with mint, sprinkle with paprika and serve with lemon wedges, olives, and yogurt, for dipping.

Nutritional information per portion: Energy 220kcal/924kJ; Protein 3.5g; Carbohydrate 31.1g, of which sugars 6g; Fat 9.9g, of which saturates 1.6g; Cholesterol 24mg; Calcium 27mg; Fibre 1.2g; Sodium 18mg.

Megadarra

This dish of rice and lentils is a classic meal for both Jews and Arabs, from Egypt and Libya to Galilee and Greece. It is often enjoyed with a bowl of vegetables, cooling yogurt, and a crisp salad.

SERVES 6–8

400g/14oz/1³/₄ cups large brown or
　　green lentils
45ml/3 tbsp olive oil
3–4 onions, 1 chopped and
　　2–3 thinly sliced
5ml/1 tsp ground cumin
2.5ml/¹/₂ tsp ground cinnamon
3–5 cardamom pods
300g/11oz/1¹/₂ cups long grain
　　rice, rinsed
250ml/8fl oz/1 cup vegetable stock
salt and ground black pepper
natural (plain) yogurt, to serve

1 Put the lentils in a pan with enough water to cover. Bring to the boil, then simmer for 30 minutes, or until tender. Skim off any scum.

2 Heat half the oil in a pan and fry the chopped onion for 5 minutes until browned. Stir in half the cumin and half the cinnamon, then add to the lentils with the cardamoms, rice and stock and mix.

3 Bring to the boil, cover and simmer until the rice is tender and the liquid has been absorbed. Season to taste.

4 Meanwhile, heat the remaining oil in another pan, then add the sliced onions and fry for about 10 minutes, or until dark brown, caramelized and crisp. Sprinkle in the remaining cumin and cinnamon just before the end of cooking.

5 To serve, pile the rice and lentil mixture on to a serving dish, then top with the caramelized onions.

6 Serve the megadarra immediately, with a spoonful of yogurt on the side.

Nutritional information per portion: Energy 353kcal/1486kJ; Protein 15.4g; Carbohydrate 63g, of which sugars 4.7g; Fat 5.1g, of which saturates 0.7g; Cholesterol 0mg; Calcium 48mg; Fibre 3.3g; Sodium 20mg.

Hatzilim pilpel

In Hebrew, the word hatzilim *means aubergines and* pilpel *means spicy and peppery. In this recipe they combine to make a fiery tomato and aubergine stew that is typical of Israeli cooking.*

SERVES 4–6

60ml/4 tbsp olive oil

1 aubergine (eggplant), cut into chunks

2 onions, thinly sliced

3–5 garlic cloves, chopped

1–2 green (bell) peppers, thinly sliced

1–2 fresh hot chillies, chopped

4 canned tomatoes, diced

5ml/1 tsp ground turmeric

pinch of curry powder or ras al hanout

cayenne pepper, to taste

400g/14oz can chickpeas, drained and
    rinsed

juice of 1/2–1 lemon

30–45ml/2–3 tbsp chopped fresh
    coriander (cilantro) leaves

salt

1 Heat half the oil in a pan, add the aubergine and fry until brown. Transfer to a sieve (strainer), standing over a bowl, and drain.

2 Heat the remaining oil in the pan, add the onions, garlic, peppers and chillies and fry until softened. Add the diced tomatoes, spices and salt, and cook, stirring, until the mixture is of a sauce consistency. Add a little water if necessary.

3 Add the chickpeas to the sauce and cook for about 5 minutes.

4 Add the drained aubergine chunks and stir until everything is evenly mixed. Cook for a further 5–10 minutes until all the flavours are well combined.

5 Add lemon juice to taste, then add the chopped coriander leaves. Leave to chill before serving.

Nutritional information per portion: Energy 220kcal/922kJ; Protein 8g; Carbohydrate 25.5g, of which sugars 13.1g; Fat 10.3g, of which saturates 1.5g; Cholesterol 0mg; Calcium 68mg; Fibre 7.8g; Sodium 172mg.

Summer squash and baby new potatoes in warm dill sour cream

This is an Israeli dish of fresh vegetables, such as courgettes and new potatoes, with spring onions, fragrant dill and a rich, buttery sour cream sauce.

SERVES 4

400g/14oz mixed squash, such as yellow
   and green courgettes (zucchini), and
   patty pan
400g/14oz tiny, baby new potatoes
pinch of sugar
40g/1¹/₂oz/3 tbsp butter

2 bunches spring onions (scallions), thinly
   sliced
1 large bunch fresh dill, finely chopped
300ml/¹/₂ pint/1¹/₄ cups sour cream or
   Greek (US strained plain) yogurt
salt and ground black pepper

1 Cut the squash into pieces about the same size as the potatoes. Put the potatoes in a pan and add water to cover, with the sugar and salt. Bring to the boil, then simmer for about 10 minutes, until almost tender. Add the squash and continue to cook until the vegetables are just tender, then drain.

2 Melt the butter in a large pan. Fry the spring onions until just wilted, then gently stir in the dill and vegetables.

3 Remove the pan from the heat and stir in the sour cream or yogurt. Return to the heat and heat gently until warm. Season with salt and pepper to taste and serve.

Nutritional information per portion: Energy 317kcal/1317kJ; Protein 5.8g; Carbohydrate 21g, of which sugars 6.1g; Fat 23.9g, of which saturates 14.8g; Cholesterol 66mg; Calcium 105mg; Fibre 2g; Sodium 104mg.

Baked winter squash in tomato sauce

This dish is Italian in origin and a favourite of the Jews of northern Italy, from around Mantua, where the most magnificent squash grow.

SERVES 4–6

45–75ml/3–5 tbsp olive oil

1kg/2¹/₂lb pumpkin or orange winter
    squash, peeled and sliced

1 onion, chopped

3–5 garlic cloves, chopped

2 x 400g/14oz cans chopped tomatoes

pinch of sugar

2–3 sprigs of fresh rosemary, stems
    removed and leaves chopped

salt and ground black pepper

1 Preheat the oven to 160°C/325°F/Gas 3. Heat 45ml/3 tbsp of the oil in a pan and fry the pumpkin slices in batches until golden brown, removing them from the pan as they are cooked.

2 Add the onion to the pan, with more oil if necessary, and fry for about 5 minutes until softened.

3 Add the garlic to the pan and cook for 1 minute.

4 Add the tomatoes and sugar to the pan and cook over a medium-high heat until the mixture is of a sauce consistency. Stir in the rosemary and season with salt and pepper to taste.

5 Layer the pumpkin slices and tomato sauce in an ovenproof dish, ending with some sauce. Bake for 35 minutes until the top is beginning to brown, and the pumpkin is tender. Serve immediately.

Nutritional information per portion: Energy 94kcal/392kJ; Protein 2.1g; Carbohydrate 7.8g, of which sugars 7g; Fat 6.2g, of which saturates 1.1g; Cholesterol 0mg; Calcium 58mg; Fibre 3g; Sodium 12mg.

Tzimmes

This is traditionally a baked dish of vegetables and dried fruit, although sometimes fresh apples and pears are added. Some tzimmes also contain meat and can be served as a main dish.

SERVES 6

250g/9oz carrots, peeled and sliced
1 sweet potato, peeled and cut
   into chunks
1 potato, peeled and cut into chunks
pinch of sugar
25g/1oz/2 tbsp butter or vegetable oil
1 onion, chopped
10 pitted prunes, halved
25g/1oz/2 tbsp currants
5 dried apricots, roughly chopped
30ml/2 tbsp honey
5–10ml/1–2 tsp chopped fresh root
   ginger
1 cinnamon stick
juice of ½ lemon
salt

1 Preheat the oven to 160°C/325°F/Gas 3. Put the carrots, sweet potato and potato into a pan of sugared and salted boiling water and cook until they are almost tender. Drain, reserving the cooking liquid, and set aside.

2 Heat the butter or oil in a large flameproof casserole, add the chopped onion and fry briefly until softened but not browned.

3 Add the cooked vegetables to the casserole and enough of the cooking liquid to cover the vegetables completely. Add the remaining ingredients. Cover and bake for 40 minutes. Towards the end of the cooking time, check the liquid in the casserole. If there is too much, remove the lid for the last 10 minutes.

VARIATION

To make meat tzimmes, braise 500g/1¼ lb beef, cut into chunks, for 1 hour until tender. In step 2 use oil rather than butter, and add the meat to the pan with the vegetables.

Nutritional information per portion: Energy 143kcal/601kJ; Protein 1.9g; Carbohydrate 26.8g, of which sugars 15.9g; Fat 3.9g, of which saturates 2.3g; Cholesterol 9mg; Calcium 36mg; Fibre 2.9g; Sodium 55mg.

Cauliflower with garlic crumbs

In Jerusalem this simple Ashkenazi dish is often eaten with meat or fish wrapped in filo pastry as the textures and flavours complement each other perfectly.

SERVES 4–6

1 large cauliflower, cut into
    bitesize florets
pinch of sugar
90ml/6 tbsp olive or vegetable oil
130g/4^{1}/$_{2}$oz/2^{1}/$_{4}$ cups dry white or
    wholemeal (whole-wheat)
    breadcrumbs
3–5 garlic cloves, thinly sliced
    or chopped
salt and ground black pepper

1 Steam or boil the cauliflower in a pan of water, to which you have added the sugar and a pinch of salt, until just tender. Drain and leave to cool.

2 Heat 60ml/4 tbsp of the olive or vegetable oil in a pan, add the breadcrumbs and cook over a medium heat, tossing and turning, until browned and crisp. Add the garlic, turn once or twice, then remove from the pan and set aside.

3 Heat the remaining oil in the pan, then add the cauliflower, mashing and breaking it up slightly as it lightly browns in the oil. (Do not overcook but just cook lightly in the oil.)

4 Add the garlic breadcrumbs to the pan and cook, stirring, until well combined and some of the cauliflower is still holding its shape. Season with salt and pepper and serve hot or warm.

Nutritional information per portion: Energy 244kcal/1016kJ; Protein 8.9g; Carbohydrate 18.8g, of which sugars 2.2g; Fat 15.3g, of which saturates 3.8g; Cholesterol 10mg; Calcium 162mg; Fibre 1.7g; Sodium 280mg.

Deep-fried artichokes

This dish is a great speciality of the Jews of Rome. The artichokes are pressed to open them, then plunged into hot oil where their leaves twist and brown, turning them into crispy flowers.

SERVES 4

2–3 lemons, halved
4–8 small globe artichokes
olive or vegetable oil, for deep-frying
salt

1 Fill a bowl with cold water and stir in the juice of one or two of the lemons. Trim the stems of the artichokes, then trim off their tough end and remove all the outer leaves. Open the leaves of one of the artichokes and trim the tops if they are sharp. If there is any choke inside, remove it. Put the artichoke in the acidulated water and prepare the remaining artichokes.

2 Put the artichokes in a pan and pour over water to cover.

3 Bring to the boil and cook over a medium-high heat for 10–15 minutes until partly cooked. Place the artichokes upside down on a baking sheet and leave to cool, then press them open gently, being careful not to tear them apart.

4 Fill a pan with oil to a depth of 5cm/2in and heat. Add one or two artichokes, with the leaves uppermost, and press down with a slotted spoon. Fry for 5–8 minutes, turning, until golden. Drain and serve.

Nutritional information per portion: Energy 132kcal/546kJ; Protein 0.6g; Carbohydrate 1.1g, of which sugars 1.1g; Fat 14g, of which saturates 1.6g; Cholesterol 0mg; Calcium 51mg; Fibre 1.4g; Sodium 75mg.

Leek fritters

These crispy fried morsels feature prominently in the Sephardi kitchen. Legend has it that these were what the fleeing Israelites were missing and longing for when they were in the desert. They are best served at room temperature with a good squeeze of lemon juice and a sprinkling of salt.

SERVES 4

4 large leeks, total weight about
    1kg/2¼lb, thickly sliced
50g/2oz/½cup coarse matzo meal
2 eggs, lightly beaten
large pinch of dried thyme or basil
freshly grated nutmeg

olive or vegetable oil, for
    shallow frying
salt and ground black pepper
lemon wedges, to serve

1 Cook the leeks in salted boiling water for 5 minutes, or until just tender and bright green. Drain and leave to cool.

2 Chop the leeks roughly. Put in a bowl and combine with the matzo meal, eggs, herbs, nutmeg and seasoning.

3 Heat 5mm/¼in oil in a frying pan. Using two tablespoons, carefully spoon the leek mixture into the hot oil. Cook over a medium-high heat until golden brown on the underside, then turn and cook the second side.

4 Drain the fritters on kitchen paper. Cook the rest of the mixture, adding oil if needed. Serve with lemon wedges and salt.

Nutritional information per portion: Energy 326kcal/1356kJ; Protein 10g; Carbohydrate 29.2g, of which sugars 5.5g; Fat 18.8g, of which saturates 2.6g; Cholesterol 95mg; Calcium 75mg; Fibre 6.2g; Sodium 40mg.

Spinach with raisins and pine nuts

Lightly cooked spinach with a little onion, olive oil, raisins and pine nuts is a typical Jewish Italian dish, which echoes the sweet-nut combination that is so popular on the Arab-influenced Sicilian table. It is universal in other Sephardi communities, for example in Greece and Turkey.

SERVES 4

50g/2oz/scant ½ cup raisins
1kg/2¼lb fresh spinach
    leaves, washed
45ml/3 tbsp olive oil
6–8 spring onions (scallions), thinly
    sliced or 1–2 small yellow or white
    onions, finely chopped
50g/2oz/scant ½ cup pine nuts
salt and ground black pepper

1 Put the raisins in a small bowl and pour over boiling water to cover. Leave to stand for about 10 minutes until plumped up, then drain.

2 Cook the spinach in a pan over a medium-high heat, with only the water that clings to the leaves after washing, for 1–2 minutes until the leaves are bright green and wilted. Remove from the heat and drain well. Leave to cool.

3 When the spinach has cooled, chop roughly with a sharp knife.

4 Heat the oil in a frying pan over a medium-low heat, then lower the heat further and add the spring onions or onions. Fry for 5 minutes, or until soft, then add the spinach, raisins and pine nuts. Raise the heat and cook for 2–3 minutes to warm through. Season to taste and serve hot or warm.

Nutritional information per portion: Energy 198kcal/824kJ; Protein 5.2g; Carbohydrate 14.3g, of which sugars 11g; Fat 13.7g, of which saturates 1.6g; Cholesterol 0mg; Calcium 226mg; Fibre 3.1g; Sodium 218mg.

Sephardi spicy cabbage with tomatoes and peppers

This dish of humble cabbage is far more exciting than you could imagine and not one to pass by. The leaves become silky, from being thinly sliced and par-boiled, and spicy and complex when cooked with Yemenite-inspired spicing.

SERVES 4–6

1 green or white cabbage, thinly sliced
30–60ml/2–4 tbsp olive oil
2 onions, chopped
5–8 garlic cloves, chopped
1/2 green (bell) pepper, chopped
2.5ml/1/2 tsp curry powder
2.5ml/1/2 tsp ground cumin
2.5ml/1/2 tsp ground turmeric
seeds from 3–5 cardamom pods
1 mild fresh chilli, chopped
400g/14oz can tomatoes
pinch of sugar
juice of 1/2–1 lemon
45–60ml/3–4 tbsp chopped fresh
   coriander (cilantro) leaves

1 Cook the cabbage in a large pan of boiling water for 5–8 minutes, or until tender. Drain the cabbage well and set aside.

2 Meanwhile, heat the oil in a frying pan, add the chopped onion and fry until softened, then add half the garlic and the green pepper and cook for 3–4 minutes, or until the pepper softens but the garlic does not turn brown.

3 Sprinkle all the spices into the pan, stir and cook for 1–2 minutes to bring out their flavour. Add the cabbage, the tomatoes and sugar, cover and cook over a low heat for 15–30 minutes until the sauce is thick.

4 Add the lemon juice and remaining garlic and cook for about 10 minutes. Stir in the chopped coriander and serve immediately.

Nutritional information per portion: Energy 81kcal/338kJ; Protein 1.9g; Carbohydrate 9.6g, of which sugars 8.3g; Fat 4.1g, of which saturates 0.6g; Cholesterol 0mg; Calcium 43mg; Fibre 2.7g; Sodium 12mg.

Israeli chopped vegetable salad

This classic salad lends itself to endless variety: add olives, diced beetroot or use lime in place of the vinegar. It is always wonderful.

SERVES 4–6

1 each red, green and yellow (bell)
    pepper, seeded
1 carrot
1 cucumber
6 tomatoes
3 garlic cloves, finely chopped
3 spring onions (scallions), sliced
30ml/2 tbsp chopped fresh coriander
    (cilantro) leaves
30ml/2 tbsp each chopped fresh dill,
    parsley and mint leaves
1/2–1 hot fresh chilli, chopped (optional)
45ml/3 tbsp extra virgin olive oil
juice of 1–1 1/2 lemons
salt and ground black pepper

1 Using a sharp knife, finely dice the red, green and yellow peppers, carrot, cucumber and tomatoes and place them in a large mixing bowl.

2 Add the garlic, spring onions, coriander, dill, parsley, mint and chilli, if using, to the chopped vegetables and toss together to combine.

3 Pour the olive oil and lemon juice over the vegetables, season with salt and pepper to taste and toss together. Chill before serving.

Nutritional information per portion: Energy 116kcal/485kJ; Protein 3g; Carbohydrate 12.2g, of which sugars 11.7g; Fat 6.5g, of which saturates 1.1g; Cholesterol 0mg; Calcium 43mg; Fibre 3.8g; Sodium 21mg.

Moroccan vegetable salad

In Israel there are many Jews of Moroccan origin who have adapted their traditional native dishes to suit the fare of Israel.

SERVES 4

1 large cucumber, thinly sliced
2 cold, boiled potatoes, sliced
1 each red, yellow and green (bell) pepper,
    seeded and thinly sliced
300g/11oz/2 2/3 cups pitted olives
1/2–1 hot fresh chilli, chopped, or
    2–3 shakes of cayenne pepper
3–5 garlic cloves, chopped
3 spring onions (scallions), sliced,
    or 1 red onion, finely chopped
60ml/4 tbsp extra virgin olive oil
15ml/1 tbsp white wine vinegar
juice of 1/2 lemon, or to taste
15–30ml/1–2 tbsp chopped fresh mint leaves
15–30ml/1–2 tbsp chopped fresh coriander (cilantro) leaves
salt (optional)

1 Arrange the cucumber, potato and pepper slices and the pitted olives on a serving plate or in a dish.

2 Sprinkle the chopped fresh chilli or cayenne pepper over the salad and season with salt, if you like. (Olives tend to be very salty so you may not wish to add any extra salt.)

3 Sprinkle the garlic, onions, olive oil, vinegar and lemon juice over the salad. Chill before serving, sprinkled with the chopped mint leaves and coriander leaves.

Nutritional information per portion: Energy 304kcal/1257kJ; Protein 2.9g; Carbohydrate 17.1g, of which sugars 5.5g; Fat 25.2g, of which saturates 3.8g; Cholesterol 0mg; Calcium 66mg; Fibre 4.2g; Sodium 1700mg.

Salad with watermelon and feta cheese

The combination of sweet and juicy watermelon with salty feta cheese is an Israeli original and was inspired by the Turkish tradition of eating watermelon with salty white cheese in the summer.

SERVES 4

30ml/2 tbsp extra virgin
    olive oil
juice of ½ lemon
5ml/1 tsp vinegar, or to taste
sprinkling of fresh thyme
pinch of ground cumin
4 large slices of watermelon, chilled
1 frisée lettuce, core removed
130g/4½oz feta cheese,
    cut into bitesize pieces
handful of lightly toasted
    pumpkin seeds
handful of sunflower seeds
10–15 black olives

1 Pour the extra virgin olive oil, lemon juice and vinegar into a bowl or jug (pitcher). Add the fresh thyme and ground cumin, and whisk until well combined. Set aside.

2 Cut the rind off the watermelon and remove as many seeds as possible. Cut the flesh into triangular-shaped chunks.

3 Put the lettuce leaves in a large bowl, pour over the dressing and toss together.

4 Arrange the dressed leaves on a large serving dish or individual plates and add the watermelon chunks, feta cheese, pumpkin and sunflower seeds and black olives. Serve the salad immediately.

Nutritional information per portion: Energy 256kcal/1066kJ; Protein 7.7g; Carbohydrate 12.9g, of which sugars 11.6g; Fat 19.7g, of which saturates 6.2g; Cholesterol 23mg; Calcium 165mg; Fibre 1.4g; Sodium 616mg.

Galilee salad of wild greens, raw vegetables and olives

Wild greens were gathered in the Galilee by necessity during times of austerity; now they are eaten for pleasure and health. Serve this salad with labneh or yogurt cheese.

SERVES 4

1 large bunch wild rocket (arugula)
1 packet mixed salad leaves
¼ white cabbage, thinly sliced
1 cucumber, sliced
1 small red onion, chopped
2–3 garlic cloves, chopped
3–5 tomatoes, cut into wedges
1 green (bell) pepper, seeded and sliced
2–3 mint sprigs, sliced or torn
30ml/2 tbsp chopped fresh parsley or dill
pinch of dried oregano or thyme
45ml/3 tbsp extra virgin olive oil
juice of ½ lemon
15ml/1 tbsp red wine vinegar
15–20 black olives
salt and ground black pepper

1 In a large salad bowl, put the rocket, mixed salad leaves, thinly sliced white cabbage, cucumber, onion and garlic and toss gently with your fingers to combine the leaves and vegetables.

2 Arrange the tomatoes, pepper, mint, fresh and dried herbs on top of the greens and vegetables. Drizzle over the oil, lemon juice and vinegar, stud with the olives, season with salt and pepper and serve.

Nutritional information per portion: Energy 126kcal/523kJ; Protein 3.4g; Carbohydrate 11g, of which sugars 10.4g; Fat 7.9g, of which saturates 1.2g; Cholesterol 0mg; Calcium 108mg; Fibre 4.3g; Sodium 338mg.

Artichokes with garlic, lemon and olive oil

This classic dish of Florence is said to be of Jewish origin. It is not only delicious as a salad, but can also be added to roasted fish, chicken or lamb during cooking.

SERVES 4

4 globe artichokes
juice of 1–2 lemons, plus extra to
**   acidulate water**
60ml/4 tbsp extra virgin olive oil
1 onion, chopped
5–8 garlic cloves, roughly chopped
**   or thinly sliced**
30ml/2 tbsp chopped fresh parsley
120ml/4fl oz/1/2 cup dry white wine
120ml/4fl oz/1/2 cup vegetable
**   stock or water**
salt and ground black pepper

1 Remove the tough artichoke leaves. Peel the tender part of the stems and cut into bitesize pieces, then put in a bowl of acidulated water. Cut the artichokes into quarters, cut out the hearts and add the hearts to the bowl.

2 Heat the oil in a pan, add the onion and garlic and fry for 5 minutes until softened. Stir in the parsley and cook for a few seconds. Add the wine, stock and drained artichokes. Season with half the lemon juice, salt and pepper.

3 Bring the mixture to the boil, then lower the heat, cover and simmer for 10–15 minutes until the artichokes are tender. Lift the artichokes out with a slotted spoon and transfer to a serving dish.

4 Bring the cooking liquid to the boil and boil until reduced to about half its volume. Pour the mixture over the artichokes and drizzle over the remaining lemon juice. Taste for seasoning and cool before serving.

Nutritional information per portion: Energy 142kcal/586kJ; Protein 1.6g; Carbohydrate 4.1g, of which sugars 1.9g; Fat 11.3g, of which saturates 1.6g; Cholesterol 0mg; Calcium 40mg; Fibre 1.6g; Sodium 47mg.

Beetroot with fresh mint

This deep red vegetable is often considered to be quintessentially Jewish, especially in Ashkenazi communities. Serve this simple and decorative salad as part of a selection of salads.

SERVES 4

4–6 cooked beetroot (beets)
5ml/1 tsp sugar
15–30ml/1–2 tbsp balsamic vinegar
juice of ¹⁄₂ lemon
30ml/2 tbsp extra virgin olive oil
1 bunch fresh mint, leaves stripped and
**   thinly sliced**
salt

1 Slice the beetroot or cut into equal-sized dice with a sharp knife. Put the beetroot in a bowl. Add the sugar, balsamic vinegar, lemon juice, olive oil and a pinch of salt and toss together to combine.

2 Add half the thinly sliced fresh mint to the salad and toss lightly until well combined. Place the salad in the refrigerator and chill for about 1 hour. Serve garnished with the remaining thinly sliced mint leaves.

Nutritional information per portion: Energy 90kcal/378kJ; Protein 1.7g; Carbohydrate 8.9g, of which sugars 8.3g; Fat 5.6g, of which saturates 0.8g; Cholesterol 0mg; Calcium 21mg; Fibre 1.9g; Sodium 66mg.

White beans with green peppers in a spicy dressing

Tender white beans are delicious in this spicy sauce with the bite of fresh, crunchy green pepper. The dish was brought to Israel by the Jews of Balkan lands, such as Turkey, Bulgaria and Greece. It is perfect for preparing ahead of time.

SERVES 4

750g/1²/₃lb tomatoes, diced
1 onion, finely chopped
¹/₂–1 mild fresh chilli, finely chopped
1 green (bell) pepper, seeded
   and chopped
pinch of sugar
4 garlic cloves, chopped

400g/14oz can cannellini beans, drained
45ml/3 tbsp olive oil
grated rind and juice of 1 lemon
15ml/1 tbsp cider vinegar or
   wine vinegar
salt and ground black pepper
chopped fresh parsley, to garnish

1 Put the tomatoes, onion, chilli, green pepper, sugar, garlic, cannellini beans, salt and plenty of ground black pepper in a large bowl and toss together until well combined.

2 Add the olive oil, grated lemon rind, lemon juice and vinegar to the salad and toss lightly to combine.

3 Chill in the refrigerator before serving, garnished with chopped parsley.

Nutritional information per portion: Energy 226kcal/947kJ; Protein 8.8g; Carbohydrate 27.6g, of which sugars 12.9g; Fat 9.6g, of which saturates 1.5g; Cholesterol 0mg; Calcium 92mg; Fibre 9g; Sodium 409mg.

Tabbouleh

This is a wonderfully refreshing, tangy salad of soaked bulgur wheat and masses of fresh mint, parsley and spring onions. Feel free to increase the amount of herbs for a greener salad. It can be served as an appetizer or as an accompaniment to a main course.

SERVES 4–6

250g/9oz/1¹/₂ cups bulgur wheat
1 large bunch spring onions (scallions),
    thinly sliced
1 cucumber, finely chopped or diced
3 tomatoes, chopped
1.5–2.5ml/¹/₄–¹/₂ tsp ground cumin
1 large bunch fresh parsley, chopped
1 large bunch fresh mint, chopped
juice of 2 lemons, or to taste
60ml/4 tbsp extra virgin olive oil
salt
olives, lemon wedges, tomato wedges,
    cucumber slices and mint sprigs,
    to garnish (optional)
cos or romaine lettuce and natural (plain)
    yogurt, to serve (optional)

1 Pick over the bulgur wheat to remove any dirt. Place it in a bowl, cover with cold water and leave to soak for 30 minutes. Turn the bulgur wheat into a sieve (strainer) and drain well, shaking to remove any excess water, then return it to the bowl.

2 Add the spring onions to the bulgur wheat, then mix and squeeze together with your hands to combine.

3 Add the cucumber, tomatoes, cumin, parsley, mint, lemon juice, oil and salt to the bulgur wheat and toss to combine.

4 Heap the tabbouleh on to a bed of lettuce and garnish with olives, lemon wedges, tomato, cucumber and mint sprigs, if you like. Serve with a bowl of natural yogurt, if you like.

Nutritional information per portion: Energy 232kcal/965kJ; Protein 5.2g; Carbohydrate 34.6g, of which sugars 2.7g; Fat 8.4g, of which saturates 1.1g; Cholesterol 0mg; Calcium 51mg; Fibre 1.4g; Sodium 12mg.

Moroccan carrot salad

Grated raw carrot salads can be found all over Israel and are often Eastern European in origin. In this intriguing variation from North Africa, the carrots are lightly cooked before being tossed in a cumin and coriander vinaigrette. It is a perfect accompaniment for a festive or everyday meal.

SERVES 4–6

3–4 carrots, thinly sliced
pinch of sugar
3–4 garlic cloves, chopped
1.5ml/¼ tsp ground cumin,
   or to taste
juice of ½ lemon
30ml/2 tbsp extra virgin
   olive oil
15–30ml/1–2 tbsp red wine vinegar or
   fruit vinegar, such as raspberry
30ml/2 tbsp chopped fresh coriander
   (cilantro) leaves or a mixture of
   coriander and parsley
salt and ground black pepper

1 Cook the carrots by either steaming or boiling in lightly salted water until they are just tender but not soft. Drain, leave for a few moments to dry, then put in a bowl.

2 Add the sugar, garlic, cumin, lemon juice, olive oil and vinegar to the carrots and toss together. Add the herbs and season. Serve immediately or leave to chill before serving.

Nutritional information per portion: Energy 53kcal/220kJ; Protein 0.6g; Carbohydrate 4.2g, of which sugars 3.9g; Fat 3.9g, of which saturates 0.6g; Cholesterol 0mg; Calcium 29mg; Fibre 1.6g; Sodium 15mg.

Tunisienne potato and olive salad

This delicious salad is favoured in North Africa. Its simplicity and zesty spicing is one of its charms. Serve this salad for lunch as an accompaniment or as an appetizer.

SERVES 4

8 large new potatoes
large pinch of salt
large pinch of sugar
3 garlic cloves, chopped
15ml/1 tbsp vinegar of your choice, such
    as a fruit variety
large pinch of ground cumin or whole
    cumin seeds

pinch of cayenne pepper or hot paprika,
    to taste
30–45ml/2–3 tbsp extra virgin
    olive oil
30–45ml/2–3 tbsp chopped fresh
    coriander (cilantro) leaves
10–15 dry-fleshed black Mediterranean
    olives

1 Chop the new potatoes into chunks. Put them in a pan, pour in water to cover and add the salt and sugar. Bring to the boil, then reduce the heat and boil gently for about 10 minutes, or until the potatoes are just tender. Drain well and leave in a colander to cool.

2 When cool enough to handle, slice the potatoes and put in a bowl.

3 Sprinkle the garlic, vinegar, cumin and cayenne or paprika over the salad. Drizzle with olive oil and sprinkle over coriander and olives. Leave to chill before serving.

Nutritional information per portion: Energy 375kcal/1581kJ; Protein 7.1g; Carbohydrate 64.5g, of which sugars 5.3g; Fat 11.6g, of which saturates 1.9g; Cholesterol 0mg; Calcium 43mg; Fibre 4.7g; Sodium 467mg.

Noodles, kugels and pancakes

Noodles were once the glory of the Ashkenazi kitchen, eaten in innumerable ways or filled to make dumplings. Kugels are the classic savoury pudding of noodles or vegetables, bound with egg and baked until firm and crispy, while pancakes – whether filled blintzes or crispy latkes – are definitively Jewish.

Kasha varnishkes

This combination of buckwheat, mushrooms and bow-shaped pasta is a classic Ashkenazi dish. To people who have not been raised on buckwheat it may taste grainy and heavy but for others, who have eaten it throughout their childhood, it is considered heavenly.

SERVES 4–6

25g/1oz dried well-flavoured
   mushrooms, such as ceps
500ml/17fl oz/2¼ cups boiling stock
   or water
45ml/3 tbsp rendered chicken fat (for a
   meat meal), vegetable oil (for a pareve
   meal) or 40g/1½oz/3 tbsp butter (for
   a dairy meal)
3–4 onions, thinly sliced
250g/9oz mushrooms, sliced
300g/11oz/1½ cups whole, coarse,
   medium or fine buckwheat
200g/7oz pasta bows
salt and ground black pepper

1 Leave the dried mushrooms to soak in half the stock for 20–30 minutes until reconstituted. Remove from the liquid, strain and reserve the liquid.

2 Heat the fat, oil or butter in a pan and fry the onions for 5–10 minutes until softened and beginning to brown. Remove to a plate, then add the sliced mushrooms to the pan and fry briefly. Add the soaked mushrooms and cook for 2–3 minutes. Return the onions to the pan and set aside.

3 In a dry frying pan, toast the buckwheat over a high heat for 2–3 minutes, stirring. Lower the heat. Stir in the remaining stock and soaking liquid, cover and cook for 10 minutes until just tender and the liquid has been absorbed.

4 Meanwhile, cook the pasta as directed on the packet until just tender, then drain. When the buckwheat is cooked, toss in the onions and mushrooms, and the pasta. Season and serve hot.

Nutritional information per portion: Energy 364kcal/1529kJ; Protein 10.3g; Carbohydrate 67g, of which sugars 4g; Fat 7.3g, of which saturates 3.6g; Cholesterol 14mg; Calcium 47mg; Fibre 2.2g; Sodium 48mg.

Italian cold pasta

This is the traditional cold pasta dish of the Italian Jewish community. The noodles are dressed with garlic, parsley and oil and eaten cold for Shabbat, the day of the week when no cooking is allowed. Serve it as a first course or as an accompaniment to a meat, fish or dairy meal.

SERVES 4

250g/9oz dried egg noodles
30ml/2 tbsp extra virgin
   olive oil
3 garlic cloves, finely chopped
60–90ml/4–6 tbsp/¹⁄₄–¹⁄₃ cup roughly
   chopped fresh parsley
25–30 pitted green olives, sliced or
   roughly chopped
salt

1 Cook the noodles in salted boiling water as directed on the packet, or until just tender. Drain and rinse under cold running water.

2 Turn the pasta into a bowl, then add the olive oil, garlic, parsley and olives and toss together. Chill overnight before serving.

Nutritional information per portion: Energy 352kcal/1476kJ; Protein 8.6g; Carbohydrate 45.3g, of which sugars 1.6g; Fat 16.4g, of which saturates 3.1g; Cholesterol 19mg; Calcium 86mg; Fibre 4.2g; Sodium 1244mg.

Pierogi

These delicious Polish dumplings of spicy mashed potato, served with melted butter and sour cream, are hearty enough to ward off the rigours of a cold winter.

SERVES 4–6

675g/1¹/₂lb baking potatoes, peeled and
   cut into chunks
50g/2oz/4 tbsp unsalted (sweet) butter,
   plus extra melted butter to serve
3 onions, finely chopped
2 eggs, lightly beaten
1 quantity of kreplach noodle
   dough (see page 132) or 250g/9oz
   packet wonton wrappers
salt and ground black pepper
chopped parsley, to garnish
sour cream, to serve

1 Cook the potatoes in a pan of salted boiling water until tender. Drain. Meanwhile, melt the butter in a pan and fry the onions for about 10 minutes, or until browned.

2 Mash the potatoes, then stir in the onions and cool. When cool, add the eggs and mix together. Season.

3 If using noodle dough, roll out and cut into 7.5cm/3in squares. Brush the edges of the dough or wrappers with a little water.

4 Place 15–30ml/1–2 tbsp of the potato filling in the centre of each square of dough or wrapper, then top with another sheet. Press the edges together to seal. Set aside.

5 Bring a large pan of salted water to the boil, then lower the heat to a simmer. Slip the dumplings into the water and cook for about 2 minutes until tender. Remove the dumplings with a slotted spoon and drain. Serve with butter and sour cream and garnish with chopped parsley.

Nutritional information per portion: Energy 364kcal/1532kJ; Protein 10.3g; Carbohydrate 55.9g, of which sugars 7.9g; Fat 12.7g, of which saturates 5.9g; Cholesterol 94mg; Calcium 55mg; Fibre 3.7g; Sodium 164mg.

Farfel

Also known as egg barley because of their size and shape, farfel are little dumplings made of grated noodle dough. In Yiddish, farfallen means fallen away, which describes the dough as it is grated.

SERVES 4 AS AN ACCOMPANIMENT

225g/8oz/2 cups plain (all-purpose) flour

2 eggs

salt

chopped parsley, to garnish

1 Put the flour, eggs and a pinch of salt in a bowl and mix. Gradually add 15–30ml/1–2 tbsp water until the dough holds together. Continue mixing the dough, until it forms a smooth, non-sticky ball. Add a little more flour if needed. Place in a covered bowl and leave to rest for at least 30 minutes.

2 On a lightly floured surface, roll the dough into a thick rope using your hands. Leave at room temperature for 2 hours to let it dry out a little.

3 Cut the dough into chunks, then grate into barley-sized pieces, using the largest holes of a grater. Lightly toss the dumplings in flour and spread on a baking sheet or greaseproof (waxed) paper to dry.

4 To cook the dumplings, bring a large pan of salted water to the boil, put in the dumplings and boil for about 6 minutes, or until just tender. Drain well and serve hot, in a bowl of chicken soup or as a side dish. Garnish with chopped parsley.

Nutritional information per portion: Energy 229kcal/969kJ; Protein 8.4g; Carbohydrate 43.7g, of which sugars 0.9g; Fat 3.5g, of which saturates 0.9g; Cholesterol 95mg; Calcium 93mg; Fibre 1.8g; Sodium 37mg.

Noodle kugel flavoured
with apple and cinnamon

This blissfully buttery noodle kugel, which is fragrant with cinnamon and apples and oozing Old Country charm, was brought to North America from Russia. It works best if flat egg noodles that are at least 1cm/^{1}/$_2$in wide are used.

SERVES 4–6

350g/12oz egg noodles

130g/4^1/$_2$oz/generous ^{1}/$_2$ cup plus
   15ml/1 tbsp unsalted (sweet) butter

2 well-flavoured cooking apples

250g/9oz/generous 1 cup cottage cheese

3 eggs, lightly beaten

10ml/2 tsp ground cinnamon

250g/9oz/1^1/$_4$ cups sugar

2–3 handfuls of raisins

2.5ml/^{1}/$_2$ tsp bicarbonate of soda
   (baking soda)

salt

1 Preheat the oven to 180°C/350°C/Gas 4. Cook the noodles in salted boiling water according to the directions on the packet, or until just tender, then drain.

2 Melt the butter, then toss it with the noodles. Coarsely grate the apples and add to the noodles, then stir in the cottage cheese, eggs, cinnamon, sugar, raisins, bicarbonate of soda and a tiny pinch of salt.

3 Turn the noodle mixture into a deep rectangular ovenproof dish, measuring about 38 x 20cm/15 x 8in, and bake for 1–1^1/$_4$ hours, until browned and crisp. Serve immediately.

Nutritional information per portion: Energy 686kcal/2889kJ; Protein 16.2g; Carbohydrate 100.6g, of which sugars 59.9g; Fat 27.1g, of which saturates 14.4g; Cholesterol 165mg; Calcium 118mg; Fibre 2.4g; Sodium 409mg.

Kreplach

The three points of these triangular stuffed pasta dumplings symbolize the three Patriarchs: Abraham, Isaac and Jacob. They are often served at festive meals.

SERVES 4

225g/8oz/2 cups plain (all-purpose)
   flour, plus extra for dusting
2 eggs
rendered chicken fat or vegetable oil
   (optional)
salt
whole and chopped fresh chives,
   to garnish

FOR THE MEAT FILLING

90ml/6 tbsp rendered chicken fat or
   vegetable oil
1 large or 2 small onions, chopped
400g/14oz leftover, pot-roasted meat,
   minced (ground) or finely chopped
2–3 garlic cloves, chopped
salt and ground black pepper

1 To make the filling, fry the onions in the fat or oil for 5–10 minutes until soft. Add the meat, garlic, salt and pepper and stir.

2 Combine the flour with the eggs and a pinch of salt. Gradually add 15–30ml/1–2 tbsp water until the dough holds together and mix until it forms a non-sticky ball. Place in a covered bowl and leave for 30 minutes.

3 Break off walnut-size pieces of dough and, on a lightly floured surface, roll out as thinly as possible. Cut the dough into squares measuring 7.5cm/3in.

4 Working one at a time, dampen the edges of each square, then place a spoonful of filling in the centre. Fold the edges of the dough to form a triangle and press together to seal. Toss in flour, then leave for 30 minutes.

5 Cook the dumplings in a pan of salted boiling water for 5 minutes until just tender, then drain. Serve, garnished with chives.

Nutritional information per portion: Energy 666kcal/2788kJ; Protein 41.4g; Carbohydrate 51.6g, of which sugars 6.5g; Fat 34.2g, of which saturates 8.5g; Cholesterol 186mg; Calcium 125mg; Fibre 3.2g; Sodium 91mg.

Potato kugel

This traditional potato accompaniment can be prepared with butter but this recipe uses
vegetable oil, which gives a much lighter, healthier result.

SERVES 6–8

2kg/4¹/₂lb potatoes
2 eggs, lightly beaten
120ml/8 tbsp medium
   matzo meal
10ml/2 tsp salt
3–4 onions, grated
120ml/4fl oz/¹/₂ cup vegetable oil
ground black pepper

1 Preheat the oven to 200°C/400°F/Gas 6. Peel the potatoes and grate finely.

2 Place the grated potatoes in a large bowl and add the beaten eggs, matzo meal, salt and ground black pepper. Mix together until well combined. Stir in the grated onions, then add 90ml/6 tbsp of the vegetable oil.

3 Pour the remaining 30ml/2 tbsp oil into a baking tin (pan) that is large enough to spread the potato mixture out to a thickness of 4–5cm/1¹/₂–2in. Heat the tin in the oven for about 5 minutes until the oil is very hot.

4 Spoon the potato mixture into the tin, letting the hot oil bubble up around the sides and on to the top a little. (The sizzling oil helps to crisp the kugel.)

5 Bake the kugel for 45–60 minutes, or until tender and golden brown and crisp on top. Serve immediately, cut into wedges.

Nutritional information per portion: Energy 361kcal/1516kJ; Protein 8g; Carbohydrate 56.2g, of which sugars 6.8g; Fat 12.8g, of which saturates 1.8g; Cholesterol 48mg; Calcium 38mg; Fibre 3.7g; Sodium 538mg.

Matzo meal and cottage cheese latkes

Cheese latkes were probably once the most revered foods in Russia, though flour, buckwheat and matzo meal latkes were more common. The cottage cheese and matzo version here was made by Russian émigrés. The cottage cheese adds a tangy flavour and slightly gooey consistency.

MAKES ABOUT 20

275g/10oz/1¼ cups cottage cheese
3 eggs, separated
5ml/1 tsp salt
250g/9oz/2¼ cups matzo meal
1 onion, coarsely grated, or
   3–5 spring onions (scallions),
   thinly sliced

2.5ml/½ tsp sugar
30ml/2 tbsp natural
   (plain) yogurt or water
ground black pepper
vegetable oil, for shallow frying
thinly shredded spring onions (scallions),
   to garnish

1 In a bowl, mash the cottage cheese. Mix in the egg yolks, half the salt, the matzo meal, onion or spring onions, sugar, yogurt or water, and pepper.

2 Whisk the egg whites with the remaining salt until stiff. Fold one-third of the whisked egg whites into the batter, then fold in the remaining egg whites.

3 Heat the oil in a heavy frying pan to a depth of about 1cm/½in, until a cube of bread added to the pan turns brown immediately. Drop tablespoonfuls of the batter into the pan; fry over a medium-high heat until the undersides are golden brown. Turn carefully and fry the second side.

4 When cooked, remove the latkes from the pan with a slotted spoon and drain on kitchen paper. Serve immediately, garnished with shredded spring onions, or keep warm in a low oven.

Nutritional information per portion: Energy 97kcal/405kJ; Protein 4.1g; Carbohydrate 10.3g, of which sugars 1g; Fat 4.6g, of which saturates 0.8g; Cholesterol 31mg; Calcium 40mg; Fibre 0.4g; Sodium 210mg.

Potato latkes

Latkes are as much a part of the Ashkenazi Chanukkah as are the candles, the dreidels, the whole celebration. Eating foods fried in oil is the tradition for Chanukkah.

SERVES 4

3 large baking potatoes, total weight
    about 675g/1¹/₂lb, peeled
2 onions, grated
60ml/4 tbsp matzo meal
5ml/1 tsp baking powder
2 eggs, lightly beaten
2.5ml/¹/₂ tsp sugar
5ml/1 tsp salt
1.5ml/¹/₄ tsp ground black pepper
vegetable oil, for shallow frying
sour cream, to serve

FOR THE SAUCE

5 green cooking apples
1 cinnamon stick
¹/₄ lemon
about 90g/3¹/₂oz/¹/₂ cup sugar
225g/8oz/2 cups cranberries

1 To make the sauce, peel, core and chop the apples and place them in a heavy pan with the cinnamon. Pare the rind from the lemon, then squeeze the lemon juice over the apples and add the lemon rind to the pan. Add the sugar, cover and cook over a low-medium heat for about 15–20 minutes, until they are just tender. Stir occasionally.

2 Add the cranberries to the pan, cover and cook for 5–8 minutes more, or until the berries pop and are just cooked. Taste for sweetness and leave to cool.

3 To make the latkes, finely grate the potatoes. Put in a sieve (strainer) and push out as much of the liquid as possible. Transfer the potato to a bowl and combine with the onions, matzo meal, baking powder, eggs, sugar, salt and pepper.

4 Heat the oil in a pan to a depth of 1cm/¹/₂in until batter sizzles when added to the pan. Fry spoonfuls of the batter for 3–4 minutes until brown and crisp. Turn and fry the second side. Remove with a slotted spoon and drain. Serve with sour cream and the cranberry apple sauce.

Nutritional information per portion: Energy 489kcal/2057kJ; Protein 9.4g; Carbohydrate 83.2g, of which sugars 44.4g; Fat 15.2g, of which saturates 2.2g; Cholesterol 95mg; Calcium 73mg; Fibre 5.9g; Sodium 61mg.

Blintzes

These thin crêpe-like pancakes are cooked on one side, stuffed, then rolled to enclose the filling and fried until crisp and brown. Unlike a crêpe batter, blintz batter is made with water.

SERVES 4

4 eggs
350ml/12fl oz/1¹/₂ cups water
pinch of salt
45ml/3 tbsp vegetable oil,
    plus extra for frying
350g/12oz/3 cups plain
    (all-purpose) flour

FOR THE FILLING
500g/1¹/₄lb/2¹/₄ cups cottage cheese
1 egg, lightly beaten
grated rind of ¹/₂–1 lemon
15ml/1 tbsp sugar
15ml/1 tbsp sour cream
30ml/2 tbsp sultanas (golden raisins)

1 For the filling, put the cottage cheese in a sieve (strainer) and drain for 20 minutes. Mash it with a fork, then add the egg, lemon rind, sugar, sour cream and sultanas and mix.

2 To make the blintzes, whisk the eggs in a bowl, then add the water, salt and oil. Whisk in the flour and beat to form a smooth batter. Heat a pancake pan, add a slick of oil, then ladle a little batter into the pan, swirling it to form a pancake.

3 When the batter has set and the edges begin to lift, flip the pancake on to a plate. Continue with the remaining batter to make 8 pancakes.

4 Place a spoonful of filling on the cooked side of a pancake and spread, leaving a gap at the top and bottom. Roll the pancake up to enclose the filling. Heat the pan, add a little oil, then fry the pancakes until the underside is golden. Turn over and fry the second side. Serve hot.

Nutritional information per portion: Energy 613kcal/2578kJ; Protein 31.9g; Carbohydrate 75.9g, of which sugars 9.3g; Fat 21.9g, of which saturates 6.4g; Cholesterol 260mg; Calcium 322mg; Fibre 2.7g; Sodium 467mg.

Breads, desserts and baking

No Bar or Bat Mitzvah kiddush would be

complete without a table of sweetmeats –

from the cookies of the Ashkenazim to the

syrupy exotic cakes of the Sephardim.

Many cakes are made without flour, to eat

during the festival of Pesach when

leavened foods are not allowed but when

festive meals are the order of the day.

Challah

Sweet, shiny challah is the traditional braided Ashkenazi bread served at celebrations. Each Shabbat, it is challah that ushers in the observances, along with wine and candles. It is said that the shape resembles the hair of a Polish maiden for whom a baker had an unrequited passion.

MAKES 2 LOAVES

15ml/1 tbsp dried active yeast
15ml/1 tbsp sugar
250ml/8fl oz/1 cup lukewarm water
500g/1¼lb/4½ cups strong white
    bread flour, plus extra if needed
30ml/2 tbsp vegetable oil

2 eggs, lightly beaten, plus 1 extra
    for glazing
pinch of sugar
salt
poppy or sesame seeds,
    for sprinkling

1 Mix together the yeast, sugar and 120ml/4fl oz/½ cup water. Sprinkle the mixture with a little flour, cover and leave for about 10–12 minutes until bubbles appear on the surface.

2 Beat 5ml/1 tsp salt, the oil and eggs into the mixture until well mixed, then add the flour, slowly at first until absorbed, then more quickly. Knead for 5–10 minutes until the mixture forms a dough that leaves the sides of the bowl. If the dough is sticky, add a little more flour and knead again. Place the dough in an oiled bowl. Cover and leave in a warm place for 1½–2 hours until doubled in size.

3 Turn the dough on to a lightly floured surface and knead gently, then return to the bowl. Cover and place in the refrigerator overnight to rise.

4 Turn the dough on to a lightly floured surface, punch down and knead until shiny and pliable. Divide the dough into two equal pieces, then divide each piece into three. Roll each into a long sausage shape.

5 Pinch the ends of three pieces together, then braid into a loaf. Repeat with the remaining dough and place on a non-stick baking sheet. Cover and leave to rise for 1 hour, or until doubled in size.

6 Preheat the oven to 190°C/375°F/Gas 5. Combine the remaining egg, the sugar and salt, and brush over the loaves, then sprinkle with the poppy or sesame seeds. Bake for 40 minutes, or until well browned. Leave to cool on a wire rack.

Nutritional information per loaf: Energy 1055kcal/4464kJ; Protein 29.8g; Carbohydrate 202.1g, of which sugars 11.6g; Fat 19.8g, of which saturates 3.4g; Cholesterol 190mg; Calcium 383mg; Fibre 7.8g; Sodium 78mg.

New York seeded corn rye sourdough

Fortunately you do not have to be Jewish to love this Eastern European Jewish bread. It is surprisingly easy to make, although you need to prepare the bread well in advance as the starter takes a few days to ferment.

MAKES 2 LOAVES

1.6kg/3¹/₂lb/14 cups unbleached strong white bread flour

7g packet easy-blend (rapid-rise) dried yeast

250ml/8fl oz/1 cup lukewarm water

60ml/4 tbsp caraway or dill seeds

15ml/1 tbsp salt

cornmeal, for sprinkling

FOR THE SOURDOUGH STARTER

250g/9oz/2¹/₄ cups unbleached strong white bread flour

7g packet easy-blend (rapid-rise) dried yeast

250ml/8fl oz/1 cup lukewarm water

FOR THE SPONGE

200g/7oz/1³/₄ cups rye flour

250ml/8fl oz/1 cup lukewarm water

1 For the starter, mix the flour and yeast together. Make a central well, stir in the water and mix. Cover and leave at room temperature for 2 days. For the sponge, mix the rye flour, starter and water together. Leave for 8 hours.

2 Combine the flour with the sponge mixture, yeast, water, caraway seeds and salt and mix to form a soft sticky dough. Turn into a bowl, sprinkle with flour, cover and leave in a warm place for 2 hours until doubled in size.

3 Punch the dough down on a floured surface. Knead for 3–4 minutes until smooth and elastic. Divide in half and shape each piece into a round loaf. Place the loaves on baking sheets sprinkled with cornmeal and score each loaf. Cover and leave in a warm place for 45 minutes until doubled in size.

4 Preheat the oven to 220°C/425°F/Gas 7. Fill a roasting pan with boiling water and place in the bottom of the oven. Bake the loaves for 35 minutes until lightly browned and hollow-sounding on the base. Cool on a wire rack.

Nutritional information per loaf: Energy 3495kcal/14863kJ; Protein 96.4g; Carbohydrate 796.5g, of which sugars 15.4g; Fat 13.4g, of which saturates 2.1g; Cholesterol 0mg; Calcium 1436mg; Fibre 31.8g; Sodium 2978mg.

Pumpernickel

Dark bread was the mainstay of most meals during the centuries of Jewish life in Poland,
Russia and the Baltic states and might be spread with butter, chicken fat or sour cream, or
simply rubbed with onion or garlic.

MAKES 2 LOAVES

65g/2¹/₂oz plain (semisweet) chocolate
   or unsweetened cocoa powder
7g packet easy-blend (rapid-rise)
   dried yeast
200g/7oz/1³/₄ cups rye flour
300g/11oz/2³/₄ cups strong
   white bread flour
5ml/1 tsp salt
2.5ml/¹/₂ tsp sugar
15ml/1 tbsp instant coffee powder
15ml/1 tbsp caraway seeds (optional)
105ml/7 tbsp warm dark beer
15ml/1 tbsp vegetable oil
90ml/6 tbsp treacle (molasses)
cornmeal, for sprinkling

1 Melt the chocolate with 50ml/2fl oz/¹/₄ cup water in a heatproof bowl set over a pan of simmering water. Set aside. Combine the yeast, flours, salt, sugar, coffee and caraway seeds, if using. Make a well, then pour in the chocolate, 175ml/6fl oz/³/₄ cup water, the beer, oil and treacle. Mix to a dough, then knead on a floured surface for 10 minutes until smooth. Put the dough in an oiled bowl and turn the dough to coat in oil. Cover and leave for 1¹/₂ hours, or until doubled in size.

2 Oil a baking sheet and sprinkle with cornmeal. Punch the dough down on a lightly floured surface. Knead for 3–4 minutes, then divide the dough and shape into two round loaves. Place on the baking sheet, cover and leave in a warm place for 45 minutes, or until doubled in size.

3 Preheat the oven to 185°C/360°F/Gas 4¹/₂. Bake for 40 minutes, or until they sound hollow when tapped on the base. Cool on a wire rack.

Nutritional information per loaf: Energy 1276kcal/5400kJ; Protein 27.3g; Carbohydrate 246.4g, of which sugars 42.4g; Fat 24.3g, of which saturates 8.6g; Cholesterol 5mg; Calcium 395mg; Fibre 9.1g; Sodium 187mg.

Bagels

These ring-shaped rolls are one of the Eastern European Jews' best contributions to the gastronomy of the world. The dough is first boiled to give it a chewy texture and then baked. The bagels can be topped with almost anything: schmears, flavoured cream cheese, lox or fresh, chopped vegetables are just a few examples.

MAKES 10 TO 12

7g packet easy-blend (rapid-rise) dried
   yeast
25ml/1¹/₂ tbsp salt
500g/1¹/₄lb/4¹/₂ cups strong
   white bread flour

250ml/8fl oz/1 cup lukewarm water
oil, for oiling
30ml/2 tbsp sugar
cornmeal, for sprinkling
1 egg yolk

1 Combine the yeast, salt and flour. Pour the lukewarm water into a separate bowl. Gradually add half the flour to the lukewarm water, beating until it forms a smooth, soft batter. Knead the remaining flour into the batter until the mixture forms a fairly firm, smooth dough.

2 Knead the dough on a floured surface for 10–20 minutes until shiny and smooth. If the dough is sticky, add a little more flour.

3 Put the dough in an oiled bowl and turn to coat it completely in the oil. Cover and leave in a warm place for 40 minutes, or until doubled in size.

4 Punch the dough down on a lightly floured surface. Knead for 3–4 minutes, or until smooth and elastic. Divide the dough into 10–12 balls. Poke your thumb through each one then, working with your fingers, open the hole to form a bagel measuring 6–7.5cm/2¹/₂–3in in diameter. Place on a floured board and leave to rise for 20 minutes, or until doubled in size.

5 Preheat the oven to 200°C/400°F/Gas 6. Bring 3–4 litres/5–7 pints/2¹/₂–3¹/₂ quarts water to the boil in a large pan and add the sugar. Lower the heat to a gentle boil. Lightly oil a baking sheet and sprinkle with cornmeal. Beat the egg yolk with 15ml/1 tbsp water. Add the bagels, one at a time, to the boiling water, until you have a single layer of bagels, and cook for 8 minutes, turning occasionally. Remove with a slotted spoon, drain and place on the prepared baking sheet.

6 Brush each bagel with the egg mixture and bake for 25–30 minutes until well browned. Cool on a wire rack.

Nutritional information per roll: Energy 157kcal/667kJ; Protein 4.2g; Carbohydrate 35g, of which sugars 3.2g; Fat 1g, of which saturates 0.2g; Cholesterol 17mg; Calcium 62mg; Fibre 1.3g; Sodium 821mg.

Pitta bread

Throughout the Mediterranean, pitta is the most commonly found bread. There are many different types, from very flat ones, to those with pockets, to a thicker cushiony one.

MAKES 12

500g/1¹⁄₄lb/4¹⁄₂ cups strong white
  bread flour, or half white and
  half wholemeal (whole-wheat)
7g packet easy-blend (rapid-rise) dried
  yeast
15ml/1 tbsp salt
15ml/1 tbsp olive oil
250ml/8fl oz/1 cup water

1 Combine the flour, yeast and salt. Mix the oil and water, then stir in half of the flour mixture, stirring until the dough is stiff. Knead in the remaining flour.

2 Place the dough in a bowl, cover and leave in a warm place for at least 30 minutes. Knead for 10 minutes, or until smooth. Put the dough in an oiled bowl, cover and leave to rise in a warm place for 1 hour, or until doubled in size.

3 Divide the dough into 12 equal-sized pieces. Flatten each piece, then roll out into a round 20cm/8in and 5mm–1cm/¹⁄₄–¹⁄₂in thick. Cover.

4 Heat a frying pan over a medium-high heat. When smoking hot, cook one piece of dough for 15–20 seconds. Turn and cook the other side for 1 minute. When bubbles start to form, turn over again. Using a dish towel, press where the bubbles have formed. Remove from the pan. Repeat with the remaining dough.

Nutritional information per pitta: Energy 150kcal/638kJ; Protein 3.9g; Carbohydrate 32.4g, of which sugars 0.6g; Fat 1.5g, of which saturates 0.2g; Cholesterol 0mg; Calcium 58mg; Fibre 1.3g; Sodium 493mg.

Onion rolls

These sweet-smelling, tender rolls are based on those found in the Ukrainian bakeries of McAllister Street in San Francisco, which used to be like a tiny shtetl.

MAKES 12–14

15ml/1 tbsp dried active yeast
15ml/1 tbsp sugar
250ml/8fl oz/1 cup lukewarm
    water
30ml/2 tbsp vegetable oil
2 eggs, lightly beaten
500g/1¼lb/4½ cups strong
    white bread flour
3–4 onions, very, very
    finely chopped
60ml/4 tbsp poppy seeds
salt

1 Mix together the yeast, sugar and water. Sprinkle with a little of the flour and leave for 10 minutes until bubbles appear on the surface. Beat in a pinch of salt, the oil and one of the eggs. Gradually add the remaining flour and knead for 5–10 minutes. Put the dough in an oiled bowl and turn to coat.

2 Leave in a warm place for 1½ hours, until doubled in size. Punch the dough down on a floured surface and knead for 3 minutes. Knead in half the onions.

3 Form into egg-sized balls, then press into rounds 1cm/½in thick. Beat the remaining egg with 30ml/2 tbsp water and a pinch of salt. Press an indentation on top of each and brush with the egg. Sprinkle over the remaining onions and poppy seeds and leave in a warm place, for 45 minutes, or until doubled in size.

4 Preheat the oven to 190°C/375°F/Gas 5. Bake for 20 minutes, until pale golden brown. Serve hot, or leave to cool.

Nutritional information per roll: Energy 161kcal/681kJ; Protein 4.6g; Carbohydrate 31.1g, of which sugars 3.3g; Fat 2.9g, of which saturates 0.5g; Cholesterol 27mg; Calcium 62mg; Fibre 1.5g; Sodium 12mg.

Coriander and cheese yeasted flatbreads

These flatbreads are salty from the halloumi cheese and are best eaten with a little unsalted butter, mixed with chopped raw garlic, or with a bowl of yogurt sprinkled with garlic, and with a mixed green salad.

MAKES 10

500g/1¼lb/4½ cups strong white
   bread flour
2 x 7g packets easy-blend
   (rapid-rise) dried yeast
5ml/1 tsp sugar
1 bunch fresh chives, chopped
60–90ml/4–6 tbsp chopped fresh
   coriander (cilantro)
45–75ml/3–5 tbsp dried onion flakes
200ml/7fl oz/scant 1 cup water
60ml/4 tbsp natural (plain) yogurt
45ml/3 tbsp olive oil
250g/9oz halloumi cheese, finely diced

1 Mix the flour, yeast, sugar, chives, coriander and onion flakes together. Add the water, yogurt and oil and mix to form a dough.

2 Knead the dough for 5–10 minutes until smooth. Put the dough in an oiled bowl, cover and leave in a warm place for 1 hour, or until doubled in size.

3 Turn the dough on to a lightly floured surface and punch down with your fists. Knead in the cheese, then knead for a further 3–4 minutes.

4 Preheat the oven to 220°C/425°F/Gas 7. Divide the dough into 10 pieces and shape each piece into a flat round 1cm/½in thick. Place the rounds on non-stick baking sheets and leave for 10 minutes, or until doubled in size.

5 Bake for 15 minutes until they are risen and golden brown. Serve at once.

Nutritional information per bread: Energy 291kcal/1222kJ; Protein 11.8g; Carbohydrate 39.4g, of which sugars 1.3g; Fat 10.2g, of which saturates 4.6g; Cholesterol 18mg; Calcium 290mg; Fibre 1.8g; Sodium 257mg.

Yemeni sponge flatbreads

These flatbreads, known as lahuhs and made from a batter, are bubbly and soft and similar to a thin crumpet. They are eaten with soups but are also good dipped into the Israeli hot sauce zchug or served with roasted tomatoes and goat's cheese.

SERVES 4

15ml/1 tbsp dried active yeast
15ml/1 tbsp sugar
500ml/17fl oz/2¼ cups lukewarm water
350g/12oz/3 cups plain
   (all-purpose) flour
5ml/1 tsp salt
50g/2oz/¼ cup butter, melted, or
   60ml/4 tbsp vegetable oil

1 Dissolve the dried yeast and a pinch of the sugar in 75ml/2½fl oz/⅓ cup of the water. Leave in a warm place for 10 minutes until frothy.

2 Stir the remaining water and sugar, the flour, salt and melted butter or oil into the yeast mixture and mix to a smooth batter. Cover and leave in a warm place for 1 hour until doubled in size.

3 Stir the thick, frothy batter and, if it seems too thick to ladle out, add a little extra water. Cover and leave in a warm place for about 1 hour.

4 Heat a non-stick frying pan. Ladle 45–60ml/3–4 tbsp of batter into the pan and cook over a low heat until the top is bubbling and the colour has changed. Remove from the pan and keep warm, or turn and cook the other side briefly, if you wish. Repeat with the remaining batter.

Nutritional information per bread: Energy 406kcal/1714kJ; Protein 8.3g; Carbohydrate 72g, of which sugars 5.3g; Fat 11.4g, of which saturates 6.7g; Cholesterol 27mg; Calcium 127mg; Fibre 2.7g; Sodium 79mg.

Tropical scented red and orange fruit salad

This fresh fruit salad, with its special colour and exotic flavour, is perfect after a rich, heavy meal. It is a lovely dish to serve at Pesach, which falls in the spring.

SERVES 4–6

350–400g/12–14oz/3–3¹/₂ cups
   strawberries, hulled and halved
3 oranges, peeled and segmented
3 small blood oranges, peeled
   and segmented
1–2 passion fruit
120ml/4fl oz/¹/₂ cup dry white wine
sugar, to taste

1 Put the strawberries and oranges into a serving bowl. Halve the passion fruit and spoon the flesh into the bowl.

2 Pour the wine over the fruit and add sugar to taste. Toss gently and then chill until ready to serve.

Nutritional information per portion: Energy 80kcal/339kJ; Protein 2.1g; Carbohydrate 15.3g, of which sugars 15.3g; Fat 0.2g, of which saturates 0g; Cholesterol 0mg; Calcium 74mg; Fibre 3.1g; Sodium 12mg.

Dried fruit compote

Compotes made using dried fruits are light, healthy and refreshing after a heavy festive meal.
They're also simple to make, and very convenient for preparing ahead of time.

SERVES 4

225g/8oz/1¹/₃ cups mixed
   dried fruit
75g/3oz/²/₃ cup dried cherries
75g/3oz/²/₃ cup sultanas
   (golden raisins)
10 prunes
10 dried apricots
hot, freshly brewed fragrant tea,
   such as Earl Grey or jasmine,
   to cover
15–30ml/1–2 tbsp sugar
¹/₄ lemon, sliced
60ml/4 tbsp brandy

1 Put the dried fruits in a bowl and pour over the hot tea. Add sugar to taste and the lemon slices. Cover with a plate, set aside and leave to cool to room temperature.

2 When the fruits have cooled sufficiently, chill in the refrigerator for at least 2 hours and preferably overnight. Just before serving, pour in the brandy and stir well.

Nutritional information per portion: Energy 189kcal/807kJ; Protein 2.6g; Carbohydrate 46.8g, of which sugars 46.8g; Fat 0.4g, of which saturates 0g; Cholesterol 0mg; Calcium 38mg; Fibre 5.3g; Sodium 20mg.

Cheese-filled Jerusalem kodafa drenched with syrup

This sweet pastry is usually made with kadaif, a shredded wheat-like pastry that can be bought ready-made. The version here uses couscous, which gives an equally delicious result.

SERVES 6

200g/7oz/1 cups couscous
500ml/17fl oz/2¹⁄₄ cups
   boiling water
130g/4oz/¹⁄₂ cup butter, cut into small
   pieces
1 egg, lightly beaten
pinch of salt
400g/14oz/1³⁄₄ cups ricotta cheese
175g/6oz cheese, such as mozzarella,
   Taleggio or Monterey Jack, grated or
   finely chopped

350ml/12fl oz/1¹⁄₂ cups
   clear honey
2–3 pinches of saffron threads
   or ground cinnamon
120ml/4fl oz/¹⁄₂ cup water
5ml/1 tsp orange flower water or
   lemon juice
50g/2oz/¹⁄₄ cup roughly chopped shelled
   pistachio nuts

1 Put the couscous in a large bowl and pour over the boiling water. Stir with a fork, then leave to soak for about 30 minutes until the water has been completely absorbed.

2 When the couscous is cool enough to handle, break up all the lumps with your fingers. Stir the butter into the couscous, then stir in the beaten egg and salt.

3 Preheat the oven to 200°C/400°F/Gas 6. Spread half the couscous into a 25–30cm/10–12in round cake tin (pan). In a bowl, combine the cheeses and 30ml/2 tbsp of the honey. Spread on top of the couscous, then top with the remaining couscous. Press down and bake for 10 minutes.

4 Put the remaining honey, the saffron and the water in a pan. Bring to the boil, then boil for 5–7 minutes, or until the liquid forms a syrup. Remove from the heat and stir in the orange flower water.

5 When the kodafa is cooked, place under the grill (broiler) and cook until it is lightly browned on top and a golden crust is formed.

6 Sprinkle the pistachio nuts on top of the kodafa. Serve warm, cut into wedges, with the syrup.

Nutritional information per portion: Energy 702kcal/2927kJ; Protein 17.6g; Carbohydrate 65.1g, of which sugars 47.6g; Fat 43g, of which saturates 22.7g; Cholesterol 123mg; Calcium 140mg; Fibre 0.9g; Sodium 344mg.

Buttered challah pudding with fruit and nuts

Leftover challah makes super bread pudding, as anyone who has eaten it will agree. If you plan to serve it after a meat meal, use fruit juice, such as pear juice, in place of the milk.

SERVES 6–8

75g/3oz/6 tbsp butter, softened, plus
extra for greasing
750ml/1¼ pints/3 cups milk
4 eggs, lightly beaten
2.5ml/½ tsp vanilla extract
2.5ml/½ tsp almond extract
1.5ml/¼ tsp salt
500g/1¼lb leftover, slightly dry challah,
thickly sliced and lightly toasted
130g/4½oz/1 cup dried cherries
3 firm, ripe pears
200g/7oz/1 cup demerara (raw) sugar
130g/4½oz/1 cup flaked almonds
cream, to serve (optional)

1 Preheat the oven to 190°C/375°F/Gas 5. Grease a 25cm/10in square or oval baking dish with a little butter.

2 Mix the milk, eggs, vanilla, almond extract and salt together in a bowl.

3 Spread the challah toast with butter, reserving 40g/1½oz/3 tbsp, then cut the challah into bitesize chunks. Add the buttered challah and dried cherries to the milk mixture and fold in gently so that all of the bread is coated in the liquid.

4 Core and dice the pears but do not peel. Layer the bread, sugar, almonds and pears in the dish, ending with a layer of sugar. Dot with butter. Bake for 40–50 minutes, or until caramelized. Serve with cream, if you like.

Nutritional information per portion: Energy 631kcal/2660kJ; Protein 17.2g; Carbohydrate 95.8g, of which sugars 63.3g; Fat 22.7g, of which saturates 7.6g; Cholesterol 122mg; Calcium 221mg; Fibre 4.1g; Sodium 491mg.

Tuscan citrus sponge

This Pesach cake comes from the Tuscan town of Pitigliano, whose rich Jewish tradition dates back to the 13th century. Made with matzo and potato flour, it is kosher for the festival.

SERVES 6–8

12 eggs, separated
300g/11oz/1½ cups caster (superfine) sugar
120ml/4fl oz/½ cup fresh orange juice
grated rind of 1 orange
grated rind of 1 lemon
50g/2oz/½ cup potato flour, sifted
90g/3½oz/¾ cup fine matzo meal or matzo meal flour, sifted
large pinch of salt
icing (confectioners') sugar, for dusting (optional)

1 Preheat the oven to 160°C/325°F/Gas 3. Whisk the egg yolks in a large bowl until pale and frothy, then whisk in the sugar, orange juice, orange rind and lemon rind.

2 Fold the sifted flours into the egg mixture. In another clean bowl, whisk the egg whites with the salt until stiff, then gently fold into the egg yolk mixture.

3 Pour the cake mixture into a deep, ungreased 25cm/10in cake tin (pan) and bake for about 1 hour, or until a cocktail stick (toothpick), inserted in the centre, comes out clean. Leave to cool in the tin.

4 When cold, turn out the cake and invert it on to a serving plate. Dust the top with a little icing sugar before serving, if you wish.

Nutritional information per portion: Energy 328kcal/1381kJ; Protein 11.1g; Carbohydrate 53.7g, of which sugars 40.5g; Fat 8.8g, of which saturates 2.3g; Cholesterol 285mg; Calcium 66mg; Fibre 0.4g; Sodium 109mg.

Classic American creamy cheesecake

There are what seems like a million cheesecake recipes, including ones flavoured with fruit or scented with lemon, but this classic version is the most tempting. It makes the perfect dessert for a Bar or Bat Mitzvah or family meal, or keep it as a standby in the freezer.

SERVES 6–8

130g/4¹/₂oz/generous ¹/₂ cup butter, melted, plus extra for greasing
350g/12oz digestive biscuits (graham crackers), finely crushed
350–400g/12–14oz/1³/₄–2 cups caster (superfine) sugar
350g/12oz/1¹/₂ cups full-fat

soft white (farmer's) cheese
3 eggs, lightly beaten
15ml/1 tbsp vanilla extract
350g/12oz/1¹/₂ cups sour cream
strawberries, blueberries, raspberries and icing (confectioners') sugar, to serve (optional)

1 Butter a deep 23cm/9in springform tin (pan). Put the biscuit crumbs and 60ml/4 tbsp of the sugar in a bowl and mix together, then add the melted butter and mix well. Press the mixture into the prepared tin to cover the base and sides. Chill for about 30 minutes.

2 Preheat the oven to 190°C/375°F/Gas 5. Using an electric mixer, food processor or wooden spoon, beat the cheese until soft. Beat in the eggs, then 250g/9oz/1¹/₂ cups of the sugar and 10ml/2 tsp of the vanilla extract.

3 Pour the mixture over the crumb base and bake for 45 minutes, or until a cocktail stick (toothpick), inserted in the centre, comes out clean. Leave to cool slightly for about 10 minutes. (Do not turn the oven off.)

4 Meanwhile, combine the sour cream and remaining sugar, to taste. Stir in the remaining vanilla extract. When the cheesecake has cooled, pour over the topping, spreading it out evenly. Return to the oven and bake for a further 5 minutes to glaze.

5 Leave the cheesecake to cool to room temperature, then chill. Serve with a few fresh strawberries, blueberries and raspberries, dusted with icing sugar, if you like.

Nutritional information per portion: Energy 634kcal/2628kJ; Protein 7.8g; Carbohydrate 31.8g, of which sugars 7.7g; Fat 53.8g, of which saturates 31.5g; Cholesterol 192mg; Calcium 137mg; Fibre 1g; Sodium 536mg.

Polish apple cake

This cake is firm and moist, with pieces of apple peeking through the top. It is based on a recipe from an old Polish lady in a Californian Lubavitcher community who always used to serve it for Shabbat.

SERVES 6–8

375g/13oz/3¼ cups self-raising
   (self-rising) flour
3–4 large cooking apples, or
   cooking and eating apples
10ml/2 tsp ground cinnamon
500g/1¼lb/2½ cups caster
   (superfine) sugar

4 eggs, lightly beaten
250ml/8fl oz/1 cup
   vegetable oil
120ml/4fl oz/½ cup
   orange juice
10ml/2 tsp vanilla extract
2.5ml/½ tsp salt

1 Preheat the oven to 180°C/350°F/Gas 4. Grease a 30 x 38cm/12 x 15in square cake tin (pan) and dust with a little of the flour. Core and thinly slice the apples, but do not peel.

2 Put the sliced apples in a bowl and mix with the cinnamon and 75ml/ 5 tbsp of the sugar.

3 In a separate bowl, beat together the eggs, remaining sugar, vegetable oil, orange juice and vanilla extract until well combined. Sift in the remaining flour and salt, then stir into the mixture.

4 Pour two-thirds of the cake mixture into the prepared tin, top with one-third of the apples, then pour over the remaining cake mixture and top with the remaining apple. Bake for about 1 hour, or until golden brown.

5 Leave the cake to cool in the tin to allow the juices to soak in. Serve the cake while still warm, cut into squares.

Nutritional information per portion: Energy 653kcal/2751kJ; Protein 7.8g; Carbohydrate 105.4g, of which sugars 70.6g; Fat 25.3g, of which saturates 3.4g; Cholesterol 95mg; Calcium 215mg; Fibre 2.1g; Sodium 210mg.

Russian poppy seed cake

This plain and simple cake is studded with tiny black poppy seeds that give it a nutty, very distinctive taste. Traditionally called mohn torte, it is the staple of Russian bakeries, where it is served with hot tea.

SERVES ABOUT 8

130g/4¹/₂oz/generous 1 cup
  self-raising (self-rising) flour
5ml/1 tsp baking powder
2.5ml/¹/₂ tsp salt
2 eggs
225g/8oz/generous 1 cup caster
  (superfine) sugar
5–10ml/1–2 tsp vanilla extract
200g/7oz/scant 1¹/₂ cups poppy
  seeds, ground
15ml/1 tbsp grated lemon rind
120ml/4fl oz/¹/₂ cup milk
130g/4¹/₂oz/generous ¹/₂ cup unsalted
  (sweet) butter, melted and cooled
30ml/2 tbsp vegetable oil
icing (confectioners') sugar, sifted, for
  dusting

1 Preheat the oven to 180°C/350°F/Gas 4. Grease and base-line a 23cm/9in springform tin (pan). Sift together the flour, baking powder and salt.

2 Using an electric whisk, beat together the eggs, sugar and vanilla extract for 4–5 minutes until pale and fluffy. Stir in the poppy seeds and then the lemon rind.

3 Gently fold the sifted ingredients into the egg and poppy seed mixture, working in three batches and alternating with the milk, then fold in the melted butter and vegetable oil.

4 Pour the mixture into the tin and bake for 40 minutes, or until firm. Cool in the tin for 15 minutes, then invert the cake on to a wire rack. Serve cold, dusted with icing sugar.

Nutritional information per portion: Energy 485kcal/2023kJ; Protein 8.3g; Carbohydrate 42.7g, of which sugars 30.5g; Fat 32.4g, of which saturates 11.4g; Cholesterol 83mg; Calcium 267mg; Fibre 2.5g; Sodium 188mg.

Pesach almond cakes

This firm biscuit-like cake has the flavour of macaroons and marzipan. It is easy to make and tastes delicious served with a cup of tea or coffee. If you can wait, the texture and flavour of the cake are improved by a few days of storage.

SERVES 16

350g/12oz/3 cups ground almonds
50g/2oz/1/2 cup matzo meal
1.5ml/1/4 tsp salt
30ml/2 tbsp vegetable oil
250g/9oz/11/4 cups sugar
300g/11oz/11/3 cups brown sugar
3 eggs, separated
7.5ml/11/2 tsp almond extract
5ml/1 tsp vanilla extract
150ml/1/4 pint/2/3 cup orange juice
150ml/1/4 pint/2/3 cup brandy
200g/7oz/13/4 cups icing
   (confectioners') sugar

1 Preheat the oven to 180°C/350°F/Gas 4. Grease a 30–38cm/12–15in square cake tin (pan). Mix the ground almonds, matzo and salt together.

2 Put the oil, sugars, egg yolks, almond extract, vanilla extract, orange juice and half the brandy in a separate bowl. Stir, then add the almond mixture to form a thick batter. (It may be lumpy.) Whisk the egg whites until stiff. Fold one-third of the egg whites into the mixture to lighten it, then fold in the rest. Pour the mixture into the tin and bake for 25–30 minutes.

3 Mix the remaining brandy with the icing sugar. If necessary, add a little water to make an icing (frosting) with the consistency of single (light) cream. Remove the cake from the oven and prick the top all over with a skewer.

4 Pour the icing over the cake, then return the cake to the oven for a further 10 minutes, or until the top is crusty.

Nutritional information per portion: Energy 415kcal/1742kJ; Protein 7.6g; Carbohydrate 54g, of which sugars 51g; Fat 17.9g, of which saturates 1.7g; Cholesterol 36mg; Calcium 97mg; Fibre 2.1g; Sodium 21mg.

Strudel

This crisp pastry roll, filled with fruit and jam, is a classic Ashkenazi sweet treat to accompany tea. No one can resist a slice of strudel served with a glass of lemon tea.

MAKES 3

250g/9oz/1 cup butter, softened
250g/9oz/generous 1 cup sour cream
30ml/2 tbsp sugar
5ml/1 tsp vanilla extract
large pinch of salt
250g/9oz/2¼ cups plain
  (all-purpose) flour
icing (confectioners') sugar, sifted, for
  dusting

FOR THE FILLING

2–3 cooking apples
45ml/3 tbsp sultanas (golden raisins)
45ml/3 tbsp soft light brown sugar
115g/4oz/1 cup walnuts, roughly chopped
5–10ml/1–2 tsp ground cinnamon
60ml/4 tbsp apricot jam or conserve

1 For the pastry, beat the butter until light and fluffy, then add the sour cream, sugar, vanilla extract and salt, and beat together. Stir the flour into the mixture, then put in a plastic bag and chill overnight or longer.

2 Preheat the oven to 180°C/ 350°F/Gas 4. For the filling, core and finely chop the apples but do not peel. Put the apples in a bowl, add the sultanas, sugar, walnuts, cinnamon and apricot jam and mix.

3 Divide the pastry into thirds. Place one third on a sheet of floured baking parchment and roll to a 45 x 30cm/18 x 12in rectangle.

4 Spread a third of the filling over the pastry, leaving a 1–2cm/½–¾in border. Roll up to enclose the filling and place on a baking sheet. Repeat with the remaining pastry and filling. Bake for 25–30 minutes until golden brown. Leave for 5 minutes, then cut into slices. Dust with icing sugar.

Nutritional information per roll: Energy 1566kcal/6519kJ; Protein 17.3g; Carbohydrate 129g, of which sugars 65.2g; Fat 112.6g, of which saturates 56.1g; Cholesterol 228mg; Calcium 274mg; Fibre 5.8g; Sodium 560mg.

Rugelach

These crisp, flaky cookies, rolled around a sweet filling, resemble a snake or croissant. They are thought to have come from Poland where they are a traditional sweet treat at Chanukkah.

MAKES 48–60

115g/4oz/¹/₂ cup unsalted (sweet) butter
115g/4oz/¹/₂ cup full-fat soft white (farmer's) cheese
15ml/1 tbsp sugar
1 egg
2.5ml/¹/₂ tsp salt
about 250g/9oz/2¹/₄ cups plain (all-purpose) flour
about 250g/9oz/generous 1 cup butter, melted
250g/9oz/2 cups sultanas (golden raisins)
130g/4¹/₂oz/generous 1 cup chopped walnuts or walnut pieces
225g/8oz/1 cup caster (superfine) sugar
10–15ml/2–3 tsp ground cinnamon

1 For the pastry, beat the butter and cheese until creamy. Beat in the sugar, egg and salt.

2 Fold the flour into the creamed mixture, a little at a time, until the dough can be worked with the hands. Continue adding the flour, kneading, until it is a consistency that can be rolled out.

3 Shape the dough into a ball, then chill for at least 2 hours or preferably overnight.

4 Preheat the oven to 180°C/350°F/Gas 4. Divide the dough into six pieces. Roll out each piece into a round about 3mm/¹/₈in thick, then brush with a little melted butter and sprinkle over the sultanas, walnuts, a little sugar and the cinnamon.

5 Cut the rounds into eight to ten wedges and roll the large side of each wedge towards the tip. Brush with butter and sprinkle with sugar. Bake for 15–30 minutes until lightly browned. Cool before serving.

Nutritional information per cookie: Energy 111kcal/464kJ; Protein 1g; Carbohydrate 10.4g, of which sugars 7.2g; Fat 7.6g, of which saturates 3.9g; Cholesterol 18mg; Calcium 16mg; Fibre 0.3g; Sodium 45mg.

Hamantashen

These triangular-shaped pastries are eaten at Purim, the festival celebrating the story of Esther, Mordecai and Haman. They can be made with a cookie dough or a yeast dough, and various sweet fillings.

MAKES ABOUT 24

115g/4oz/¹/₂ cup unsalted (sweet)
   butter, at room temperature
250g/9oz/1¹/₄ cups sugar
30ml/2 tbsp milk
1 egg, beaten
5ml/1 tsp vanilla extract
pinch of salt
200–250g/7–9oz/1¹/₂–2¹/₄ cups plain
   (all-purpose) flour
icing (confectioners') sugar, for dusting

FOR THE APRICOT FILLING

250g/9oz/generous 1 cup dried
   apricots
1 cinnamon stick
45ml/3 tbsp sugar

1 Cream the butter and sugar until pale and fluffy. In another bowl mix together the milk, egg, vanilla and salt. Sift the flour into a third bowl.

2 Beat the creamed butter mix with one-third of the flour, then gradually add the remaining flour, in three batches, alternating with the milk mixture. It should be the consistency of a loose shortbread dough. Chill for 1 hour.

3 For the apricot filling, put the apricots, cinnamon stick and sugar in a pan and add enough water to cover. Heat gently, then simmer for 15 minutes, or until the apricots are tender and most of the liquid has evaporated. Remove the cinnamon, then purée the apricots in a food processor with a little of the cooking liquid until they form a consistency like thick jam.

4 Preheat the oven to 180°C/350°F/Gas 4. Roll out the dough to a thickness of 3–5mm/¹/₈–¹/₄in, then cut into rounds 7.5cm/3in in diameter. Place 15–30ml/1–2 tbsp of filling in the centre of each round, then pinch the pastry together to form three corners, leaving a little of the filling showing in the middle of the pastry. Bake for 15 minutes, or until pale golden. Serve dusted with icing sugar.

Nutritional information per pastry: Energy 202kcal/852kJ; Protein 3.1g; Carbohydrate 32.3g, of which sugars 25.9g; Fat 7.6g, of which saturates 3.1g; Cholesterol 19mg; Calcium 78mg; Fibre 2g; Sodium 44mg.

Lekach

This classic honey cake is richly spiced, redolent of ginger, cinnamon and other sweet, aromatic scents. For this reason it is eaten at Rosh Hashanah in the hope of a sweet new year.

SERVES 8

175g/6oz/1¹/₂ cups plain
   (all-purpose) flour
75g/3oz/¹/₃ cup caster
   (superfine) sugar
2.5ml/¹/₂ tsp ground ginger
2.5–5ml/¹/₂–1 tsp ground cinnamon
5ml/1 tsp mixed (apple pie) spice
5ml/1 tsp bicarbonate of soda
   (baking soda)
225g/8oz/1 cup clear honey
60ml/4 tbsp vegetable or olive oil
grated rind of 1 orange
2 eggs
75ml/5 tbsp orange juice
10ml/2 tsp chopped fresh root ginger, or
   to taste

1 Preheat the oven to 180°C/350°F/Gas 4. Line a rectangular baking tin (pan), measuring 25 x 20 x 5cm/10 x 8 x 2in, with baking parchment. Mix together the flour, sugar, ginger, cinnamon, mixed spice and bicarbonate of soda.

2 Make a well in the centre of the flour mixture and pour in the clear honey, vegetable or olive oil, orange rind and eggs. Using a wooden spoon or electric whisk, beat until smooth, then add the orange juice. Stir in the ginger.

3 Pour the cake mixture into the tin, then bake for about 50 minutes, or until firm to the touch.

4 Leave the cake to cool in the tin, then turn out and wrap tightly in foil. Store at room temperature for 2–3 days before serving to allow the flavours of the cake to mature.

Nutritional information per portion: Energy 264kcal/1115kJ; Protein 3.8g; Carbohydrate 49.1g, of which sugars 32.4g; Fat 7.2g, of which saturates 1.1g; Cholesterol 48mg; Calcium 45mg; Fibre 0.7g; Sodium 23mg.

Tunisian almond cigars

These pastries are a great favourite of the Jews from North Africa, especially Tunisia. Serve them with a small cup of fragrant mint tea or strong, dark coffee.

MAKES 8–12

250g/9oz almond paste
1 egg, lightly beaten
15ml/1 tbsp rose water or orange
    flower water
5ml/1 tsp ground cinnamon
1.5ml/¼ tsp almond extract
8–12 sheets filo pastry
melted butter, for brushing
icing (confectioners') sugar
    and ground cinnamon,
    for dusting
mint tea or black coffee, to serve

1 Knead the almond paste until soft, then put in a bowl, and mix in the egg, flower water, cinnamon and almond extract. Chill for 1–2 hours.

2 Preheat the oven to 190°C/375°F/Gas 5. Lightly grease a baking sheet with butter. Place a sheet of filo pastry on a piece of baking parchment, keeping the remaining pastry covered with a damp cloth, and brush with the melted butter.

3 Shape 30–45ml/2–3 tbsp of the filling mixture into a cylinder and place at one end of the pastry. Fold the pastry over to enclose the ends of the filling, then roll up to form a cigar shape. Place on the baking sheet and make 7–11 more cigars in the same way.

4 Bake the pastries for about 15 minutes, or until golden. Leave to cool, then dust with sugar and cinnamon, and serve with tea or coffee.

Nutritional information per pastry: Energy 109kcal/458kJ; Protein 2.2g; Carbohydrate 18.9g, of which sugars 14.2g; Fat 3.2g, of which saturates 0.4g; Cholesterol 16mg; Calcium 25mg; Fibre 0.6g; Sodium 10mg.

Mandelbrot

These crisp, twice-baked biscuits, studded with almonds, are similar to Italian almond biscotti. They were probably brought to Italy by the Jews of Spain, who then took them to Eastern Europe.

MAKES 24–36

375g/13oz/3¼ cups plain
    (all-purpose) flour
115g/4oz/1 cup ground almonds
5ml/1 tsp bicarbonate of soda
    (baking soda)
1.5ml/¼ tsp salt
3 eggs
250g/9oz/1¼ cups caster
    (superfine) sugar
grated rind of 1 lemon
5ml/1 tsp almond extract
5ml/1 tsp vanilla extract
130g/4½oz/1 cup blanched almonds,
    roughly chopped

1 Preheat the oven to 180°C/ 350°F/Gas 4. Lightly grease two baking sheets. Sift together the flour, ground almonds, bicarbonate of soda and salt.

2 Beat together the eggs and sugar for about 5 minutes, or until light and fluffy, then beat in the lemon rind and almond and vanilla extracts. Slowly add the flour and ground almonds, a little at a time, mixing until well blended. Add the chopped almonds and mix well until evenly combined.

3 Turn the mixture on to a floured surface and knead for 5 minutes. Divide the dough into two pieces and form each into a long, flat loaf. Bake for 35 minutes until browned.

4 Remove from the oven and leave to cool slightly. When cool, cut them into 1cm/½in diagonal slices.

5 Return the slices to the oven and bake for 6–7 minutes until the undersides are golden and flecked with brown. Turn over and bake for 6–7 minutes more. Leave to cool.

Nutritional information per biscuit: Energy 111kcal/466kJ; Protein 3g; Carbohydrate 15.8g, of which sugars 7.7g; Fat 4.4g, of which saturates 0.5g; Cholesterol 16mg; Calcium 37mg; Fibre 0.8g; Sodium 8mg.

Pomerantzen

This candied citrus peel is a speciality of Jews whose origins lie in Germany. It can be chopped and added to cakes, or served as a sweetmeat, coated in sugar or chocolate.

SERVES 4–6

3 grapefruits and 5–6 oranges or
    6–8 lemons, unwaxed
300g/11oz/1¾ cups sugar
300ml/½ pint/1¼ cups water
30ml/2 tbsp golden (light corn) syrup
caster (superfine) sugar (optional)

1 Peel the fruit carefully, in large strips. Put the peels in a pan of water and bring to the boil. Simmer for 20 minutes, then drain.

2 When the peels are cool, scrape off as much of the white pith as possible. Cut the peel lengthways into narrow strips.

3 Put the sugar, water and syrup in a pan and bring to the boil. When clear, add the peels; simmer for 1 hour until translucent. Do not burn.

4 Stand a rack over a baking sheet. Remove the peels from the pan and arrange them on the rack. Leave to dry for 2–3 hours, then put in a plastic container, cover and store in the refrigerator until required.

5 If coating with sugar, cover a large flat plate with caster sugar and toss the drained peels in it. Leave for 1 hour. Sprinkle with sugar again and place in a covered container. Store in a cool, dry place for 2 weeks or chill for 2 months.

Nutritional information per portion: Energy 116kcal/492kJ; Protein 0.2g; Carbohydrate 29.6g, of which sugars 29.6g; Fat 0.5g, of which saturates 0g; Cholesterol 0mg; Calcium 65mg; Fibre 2.4g; Sodium 140mg.

Pickles and condiments

Kosher dill pickles, the well-known mini cucumbers flavoured with garlic, are a deli treat brought to America from Eastern Europe, and are hugely popular. But there is a wide variety of other pickles and condiments, from pink pickled turnips to the golden mixed vegetables of the Sephardi kitchen.

Preserved lemons

These are widely used in Middle Eastern cooking. The interesting thing about preserved lemons is that you actually only eat the peel, which contains the essential flavour of the lemon. Traditionally whole lemons are preserved but this recipe uses lemon wedges which can be packed much more easily into jars.

MAKES ABOUT 2 JARS

10 unwaxed lemons
about 200ml/7fl oz/scant 1 cup fresh
**   lemon juice or a combination**
**   of fresh and preserved**
boiling water
sea salt

1 Wash the lemons well and cut each into six to eight wedges. Press a generous amount of salt into the cut surfaces, pushing it into every crevice.

2 Pack the salted lemon wedges into two 1.2 litre/2 pint sterilized jars. To each jar, add 30–45ml/2–3 tbsp salt and 90ml/6 tbsp lemon juice, then top up with boiling water, to cover the lemons. (If using larger jars, use more lemon juice and less boiling water.)

3 Cover the jars and leave to stand for 2–4 weeks before serving.

4 To serve, rinse the preserved lemons well to remove some of the salty flavour, then pull off the flesh and discard. Cut the lemon peel into strips or leave in chunks and use as desired.

COOK'S TIP
The salty, well-flavoured juice that is used to preserve the lemons can be added to salads or hot sauces, such as zchug, horef and harissa.

Nutritional information per jar: Energy 48kcal/198kJ; Protein 2.5g; Carbohydrate 8g, of which sugars 8g; Fat 0.8g, of which saturates 0.3g; Cholesterol 0mg; Calcium 213mg; Fibre 0g; Sodium 13mg.

Torshi

The pickled turnips, deep rich red in their beetroot-spiked brine, not only look gorgeous in their jars but also make a delicious pickle to add to dishes like falafel or even as part of an assortment of appetizers before a main meal.

MAKES ABOUT 4 JARS

1kg/2¼lb young turnips
3–4 raw beetroot (beets)
about 45ml/3 tbsp kosher salt or coarse
**   sea salt**
about 1.5 litres/2½ pints/
**   6¼ cups water**
juice of 1 lemon

1 Wash the turnips and beetroot, but do not peel, then cut into slices 5mm/¼in thick. Put the salt and water into a bowl, stir and leave until the salt has dissolved. Sprinkle the beetroot with lemon juice and place in the bases of four 1.2 litre/ 2 pint sterilized jars.

2 Top the beetroot with the turnips, packing them in very tightly. Carefully pour over the brine, making sure that the vegetables are completely covered. Seal the jars and leave them to stand in a cool, dry place for 7 days before serving.

Nutritional information per jar: Energy 85kcal/361kJ; Protein 3.5g; Carbohydrate 17.5g, of which sugars 16.5g; Fat 0.8g, of which saturates 0g; Cholesterol 0mg; Calcium 136mg; Fibre 7.4g; Sodium 4508mg.

Chrain

This Ashkenazi horseradish and beetroot sauce is often eaten at Pesach, for which horseradish is one of the traditional bitter flavours. However, it is a delicious accompaniment to gefilte fish, fried fish patties or roasted meat at any time of the year.

SERVES 8

150g/5oz grated fresh horseradish
2 cooked beetroot (beets), grated
about 15ml/1 tbsp sugar
15–30ml/1–2 tbsp red wine vinegar
salt

1 Put the horseradish and beetroot in a bowl and mix together, then season with sugar, vinegar and salt to taste.

2 Spoon the sauce into a sterilized jar, packing it down firmly, and seal. Store in the refrigerator, where it will keep for up to 2 weeks.

Nutritional information per portion: Energy 18kcal/74kJ; Protein 0.5g; Carbohydrate 4g, of which sugars 3.9g; Fat 0.1g, of which saturates 0g; Cholesterol 0mg; Calcium 14mg; Fibre 0.7g; Sodium 17mg.

Turkish green olive and tomato relish

This relish of green olives in a sauce of tomatoes and sweet peppers is wonderful served at a buffet with a selection of salads.

SERVES 10

45ml/3 tbsp extra virgin olive oil
1 green (bell) pepper, chopped or sliced
1 red (bell) pepper, chopped or sliced
1 onion, chopped
2–3 mild, large red and green chillies, thinly sliced
1–2 hot, small chillies, chopped or thinly sliced (optional)
5–7 garlic cloves, roughly chopped or thinly sliced
5–7 tomatoes, quartered or diced
5ml/1 tsp curry powder or hawaij
1.5ml/¼ tsp ground cumin
1.5ml/¼ tsp turmeric
large pinch of ground ginger
15ml/1 tbsp tomato purée (paste)
juice of ¼ lemon, or to taste
200g/7oz/1¾ cups pitted or pimiento-stuffed green olives

1 Heat the oil in a pan and fry the peppers, onion and chillies for 5–10 minutes, or until softened.

2 Add the garlic and tomatoes and fry for 2–3 minutes, until the tomatoes have become the consistency of a sauce, then add the curry powder, the cumin, turmeric, ginger and tomato purée. Remove from the heat.

3 Stir in the lemon juice, then add the olives. Leave to cool, then chill, preferably overnight, before serving.

Nutritional information per portion: Energy 72kcal/299kJ; Protein 1g; Carbohydrate 4.3g, of which sugars 4g; Fat 5.8g, of which saturates 0.9g; Cholesterol 0mg; Calcium 20mg; Fibre 1.7g; Sodium 456mg.

Chopped vegetable salad relish

This relish mixes the freshness and crunchiness of the salads enjoyed by Arabs with the chopped salads adored by Eastern Europeans.

SERVES 4

2–3 ripe tomatoes, finely chopped
½ cucumber, finely chopped
½ green (bell) pepper,
    finely chopped
1–2 garlic cloves, chopped
2 spring onions (scallions), sliced
30ml/2 tbsp finely chopped
    fresh mint, dill or coriander (cilantro) leaves
30ml/2 tbsp finely chopped
    fresh parsley
grated rind and juice of 1 lemon
⅛ red cabbage, chopped (optional)
salt

1 Put the tomatoes, cucumber, pepper, garlic, spring onions, herbs and lemon rind and juice together in a large serving bowl. Mix together well, then leave to chill until ready to serve.

2 If using red cabbage, add to the relish just before serving, as its colour will run and spoil the fresh and vibrant colours of all the other vegetables.

3 Add a little salt to taste and stir to mix until evenly combined. Serve immediately.

Nutritional information per portion: Energy 30kcal/126kJ; Protein 1.2g; Carbohydrate 5.6g, of which sugars 5.4g; Fat 0.5g, of which saturates 0.1g; Cholesterol 0mg; Calcium 14mg; Fibre 1.6g; Sodium 10mg.

Tahini sauce

Made of ground sesame seeds and flavoured with garlic and lemon juice, this makes a delicious dip, served with pitta bread, and can also be thinned with water and spooned over falafel.

SERVES 4–6

150g/5oz/²⁄₃ cup tahini
3 garlic cloves, finely chopped
juice of 1 lemon
1.5ml/¼ tsp ground cumin
small pinch of ground coriander
small pinch of curry powder
50ml/2fl oz/¼ cup water
cayenne pepper
salt

FOR THE GARNISH

15ml/1tbsp extra virgin olive oil
chopped fresh coriander (cilantro) leaves
    or parsley
handful of olives
a few chillies or a hot pepper sauce

1 Put the tahini and garlic in a food processor or bowl and mix together well. Stir in the lemon juice, cumin, ground coriander and curry powder.

2 Slowly add the water to the tahini, beating all the time. The mixture will thicken, then become thin. Season with cayenne pepper and salt.

3 To serve, spread the mixture on to a serving plate, individual plates or into a shallow bowl. Drizzle over the oil and sprinkle with the other garnishes.

COOK'S TIP

Tahini sauce forms the basis of many of the salads and dips found in Israel and the Middle East.

Nutritional information per portion: Energy 175kcal/725kJ; Protein 5.2g; Carbohydrate 1.2g, of which sugars 0.3g; Fat 16.7g, of which saturates 2.4g; Cholesterol 0mg; Calcium 184mg; Fibre 2.5g; Sodium 7mg.

Instant Sephardi pickle of mixed vegetables

You will find this pickle on falafel stands throughout Israel and on Sephardi tables throughout the world. It is spiced with different flavours but always crisp and tangy.

SERVES 12

½ cauliflower, cut into florets

2 carrots, sliced

2 celery sticks, thinly sliced

¼–½ cabbage, thinly sliced

115g/4oz/1 cup runner (green) beans, cut
    into bitesize pieces

6 garlic cloves, sliced

1–4 fresh chillies, whole or sliced

30–45ml/2–3 tbsp sliced fresh
    root ginger

1 red (bell) pepper, sliced

2.5ml/½ tsp turmeric

105ml/7 tbsp white wine vinegar

15–30ml/1–2 tbsp sugar

60ml/4 tbsp olive oil

juice of 2 lemons

salt

1 Toss the cauliflower, carrots, celery, cabbage, beans, garlic, chillies, ginger and pepper with salt and leave to stand in a colander for 4 hours.

2 Transfer the salted vegetables to a bowl and add the turmeric, vinegar, sugar to taste, the oil and lemon juice. Toss to combine, then add enough water to balance the flavours.

3 Cover and chill for at least 1 hour, or until ready to serve.

COOK'S TIP
This spicy pickle can be stored in the refrigerator for up to 2 weeks.

Nutritional information per portion: Energy 78kcal/321kJ; Protein 1.3g; Carbohydrate 5.2g, of which sugars 5g; Fat 5.8g, of which saturates 0.9g; Cholesterol 0mg; Calcium 23mg; Fibre 1.5g; Sodium 11mg.

Horef

The word horef is translated from Hebrew as hot pepper and here, in this Sephardi relish, the peppers are simmered with mild ones, as well as tomatoes and fragrant spices.

SERVES 4–6

45ml/3 tbsp olive oil
1 green (bell) pepper, chopped
    or sliced
2–3 mild, large chillies,
    thinly sliced
1–2 hot, small chillies, chopped
    or thinly sliced (optional)
5–7 garlic cloves, roughly chopped
    or thinly sliced
5–7 tomatoes, quartered or diced
5ml/1 tsp curry powder or hawaij
seeds from 3–5 cardamom pods
large pinch of ground ginger
15ml/1 tbsp tomato purée (paste)
juice of 1/4 lemon
salt

1 Heat the olive oil in a large, heavy pan, add the chopped or sliced green pepper, large and small chillies and garlic. Fry over a medium-high heat, stirring, for about 10 minutes, or until the peppers are softened. (Be careful not to let the garlic brown.)

2 Add the tomatoes, curry powder or hawaij, cardamom seeds and ginger to the pan, and cook until the tomatoes have softened to a sauce. Stir the tomato purée and lemon juice into the mixture, season with salt and leave to cool. Chill until ready to serve.

Nutritional information per portion: Energy 79kcal/328kJ; Protein 1.3g; Carbohydrate 5.4g, of which sugars 5.3g; Fat 6g, of which saturates 0.9g; Cholesterol 0mg; Calcium 12mg; Fibre 1.5g; Sodium 17mg.

Harissa

This recipe is a quick version of harissa, the North African chilli sauce that's terrific to add to couscous or drizzle on soups. If serving with couscous, use stock from the couscous stew.

SERVES 4–6

45ml/3 tbsp paprika
2.5–5ml/1/2–1 tsp cayenne pepper
1.5ml/1/4 tsp ground cumin
250ml/8fl oz/1 cup water or stock
juice of 1/4–1/2 lemon
2–3 pinches of caraway
    seeds (optional)
salt
15ml/1 tbsp chopped coriander (cilantro) leaves, to serve

1 Put the paprika, cayenne, ground cumin, and water or stock in a large, heavy pan and season with salt to taste.

2 Bring the spice mixture to the boil, then immediately remove from the heat.

3 Stir the lemon juice and caraway seeds, if using, into the hot spice mixture and leave to cool.

4 Just before serving, pour the sauce into a serving dish and sprinkle with the chopped coriander leaves.

Nutritional information per portion: Energy 22kcal/92kJ; Protein 1.1g; Carbohydrate 2.7g, of which sugars 0g; Fat 1g, of which saturates 0.2g; Cholesterol 0mg; Calcium 14mg; Fibre 0g; Sodium 3mg.

Coriander, coconut and tamarind chutney

Cooling fragrant chutneys made with fresh coriander and mint are beloved of the Indian Jewish community. This delicious blend of coriander, mint and coconut, with chilli, tamarind and dates, is a traditional condiment for the Bene Israel, one of the three major groups of Indian Jews.

MAKES ABOUT 450G/1LB/ 2 CUPS

30ml/2 tbsp tamarind paste

30ml/2 tbsp boiling water

1 large bunch fresh coriander (cilantro), roughly chopped

1 bunch fresh mint, roughly chopped

8 pitted dates, roughly chopped

75g/3oz dried coconut, coarsely grated

2.5cm/1in piece fresh root ginger, chopped

3–5 garlic cloves, chopped

2–3 fresh chillies, chopped

juice of 2 limes or lemons

about 5ml/1 tsp sugar

salt

30–45ml/2–3 tbsp water (for a meat meal) or yogurt (for a dairy meal), to serve

1 Place the tamarind paste in a jug (pitcher) or bowl and pour over the boiling water. Stir thoroughly until the paste is completely dissolved and set aside.

2 Place the fresh coriander, mint and pitted dates in a food processor and process briefly until finely chopped. Alternatively, chop finely by hand using a sharp knife. Place in a bowl.

3 Add the coconut, ginger, garlic and chillies to the chopped herbs and dates and stir in the tamarind. Season with citrus juice, sugar and salt. Spoon the chutney into sterilized jars, seal and chill.

4 To serve, thin the chutney slightly with the water, if serving with a meat meal, or with yogurt for a dairy meal.

Nutritional information per portion: Energy 536kcal/2232kJ; Protein 10.1g; Carbohydrate 47g, of which sugars 39.5g; Fat 35.5g, of which saturates 29.8g; Cholesterol 0mg; Calcium 144mg; Fibre 6.5g; Sodium 39mg.

Fragrant Persian halek

This halek is fragrant with rose water, cinnamon and nutmeg as well as the sweet flavours of dried fruits and nuts, which are so beloved by Persian Jews. Keep chilled in the refrigerator until you are ready to serve it.

SERVES ABOUT 10

60ml/4 tbsp blanched almonds
60ml/4 tbsp unsalted pistachio nuts
60ml/4 tbsp walnuts
15ml/1 tbsp skinned hazelnuts
30ml/2 tbsp unsalted shelled pumpkin
    seeds
90ml/6 tbsp raisins, chopped
90ml/6 tbsp pitted prunes, diced
90ml/6 tbsp dried apricots, diced
60ml/4 tbsp dried cherries
sugar or honey, to taste
juice of 1/2 lemon
30ml/2 tbsp rose water
seeds from 4–5 cardamon pods
pinch of ground cloves
pinch of freshly grated nutmeg
1.5ml/1/4 tsp ground cinnamon
fruit juice of choice, if necessary

1 Roughly chop the almonds, pistachio nuts, walnuts, hazelnuts and pumpkin seeds and put in a large bowl.

2 Add the chopped raisins, prunes, apricots and cherries to the nuts and seeds and toss to combine. Stir in sugar or honey to taste and mix well until thoroughly combined.

3 Add the lemon juice, rose water, cardamom seeds, cloves, nutmeg and cinnamon to the fruit and nut mixture and mix until thoroughly combined.

4 If the halek is too thick, add a little fruit juice to thin the mixture. Pour into a serving bowl, cover and chill until ready to serve.

Nutritional information per portion: Energy 207kcal/863kJ; Protein 5.1g; Carbohydrate 14.9g, of which sugars 14.5g; Fat 14.6g, of which saturates 1.4g; Cholesterol 0mg; Calcium 66mg; Fibre 2.8g; Sodium 42mg.

Zchug

This is the Yemenite chilli sauce that has become Israel's national seasoning. It is hot with chillies, pungent with garlic, and fragrant with exotic cardamom. Eat it with rice, couscous, soup, chicken or other meats. It can be stored in the refrigerator for up to 2 weeks.

**MAKES ABOUT
475ML/16FL OZ/2 CUPS**

5–8 garlic cloves, chopped
2–3 medium-hot chillies, such
    as jalapeño
5 fresh or canned tomatoes, diced
1 small bunch coriander (cilantro),
    roughly chopped
1 small bunch parsley, chopped

30ml/2 tbsp extra virgin olive oil
10ml/2 tsp ground cumin
2.5ml/1/2 tsp turmeric
2.5ml/1/2 tsp curry powder
seeds from 3–5 cardamom pods
juice of 1/2 lemon
pinch of sugar, if necessary
salt

1 Put the garlic, chillies, tomatoes, coriander, parsley, olive oil, cumin, turmeric, curry powder, cardamom seeds and lemon juice into a food processor or blender. Process until well combined, then season with the sugar and salt.

2 Pour the sauce into a serving bowl, cover and chill in the refrigerator until ready to serve.

Nutritional information per portion: Energy 326kcal/1361kJ; Protein 7.1g; Carbohydrate 21.4g, of which sugars 17.5g; Fat 24.3g, of which saturates 3.7g; Cholesterol 0mg; Calcium 142mg; Fibre 8.6g; Sodium 63mg.

The Jewish kitchen

The foods of the Jewish table are global

by nature, reflecting the flavours of the

countries where Jews have settled. They

also have their roots in tradition.

Ashkenazi and Sephardi foods are very

different but cross-cultural marriages

and the intermingling of different people

have blurred the boundaries.

History

Exile has been a common thread throughout Jewish history. It is this, linked with intrinsic religious and cultural considerations, that has been a major factor in developing a cuisine that is so diverse. As communities fled from one country to another, they took with them their culinary traditions but also adopted new ones along the way.

THE JEWISH DIASPORA

With the destruction by the Romans of the Second Temple in Jerusalem in 70CE (AD), the Jews were banished from their holy city. Since that date, they have travelled the world, establishing communities before being forced to flee once more.

Jews spread to nearly every corner of the globe and this dispersal or diaspora has helped to create the cultural and liturgical differences that exist within a single people. Following the dispersal, two important Jewish communities were established, which still define the two main Jewish groups that exist today: the Sephardim and the Ashkenazim, who each have their own individual culture, cuisine and liturgy.

The first of these communities was in Iberia and was called Sepharad after a city in Asia Minor mentioned in Obadiah 20. The second was in the Rhine River Valley and was called Ashkenaz, after a kingdom on the upper Euphrates.

BELOW: *A painting by Francesco Hayez of 1867 of the destruction of the Jewish Temple in Jerusalem by the Romans in 70CE (AD).*

THE SEPHARDIM

Jews who settled in Iberia spoke Ladino, a dialect of Castilian Spanish written in Hebrew script. In many respects, their lifestyle was not so very different from that of their Arab neighbours, who had a similar outlook of generous hospitality.

The food the Sephardi Jews ate, and the way they cooked it, was a blend of their own heritage and dietary laws, with distinct influences from the Iberian and Arabic culinary tradition. What emerged was a cuisine rich with the flavours of the region.

At its heart, Sephardi cooking still has the warm undertones of Spain: it is olive oil-based, rich with fish from the sea and the vegetables of a warm climate, fragrant with garlic, herbs and spices. When meat is used, it is usually lamb.

The Sephardim also introduced their own influences on the Iberian and Arab cuisines. Even today, if you enquire in Andalucía in Spain as to what have been the major influences on their cuisine, the Jewish contribution will be acknowledged alongside that of the Moors.

Sephardi cooking reflected Sephardi life: sensual and imbued with life's pleasures. This attitude went a lot further than just the food. It is reflected in all the celebrations for life's happy occasions too. For instance, in Sephardi tradition, a typical wedding celebration lasted for two weeks, and a Brit Milah or Bar Mitzvah celebration lasted for a week. These old traditions still live on today.

INTO EXILE AGAIN

The Sephardim, who had flourished in Spain for centuries, then found the tide beginning to turn against them. Shortly before the end of the 14th century, antagonism erupted into violent riots and thousands of Jews were massacred.

Many of those who survived were forced, on pain of death, to convert. These Jews were known as *conversos* or – less politely – *marranos*, which means pork eaters. They and their families often continued their religious practices in secret. Traditional food, and the rituals associated with it, became a source of comfort for the *conversos* and a reminder of their history.

For a few decades these clandestine Jews flourished but they were a thorn in the flesh of the Spanish rulers and led to the Spanish Inquisition at the end of the 15th century. In 1492 all the remaining Jews in Spain were expelled. They scattered to North Africa, Europe, the Middle East and the New World. With each migration, Sephardi Jews encountered new flavours, which they introduced into their own cooking.

THE ASHKENAZIM

The Jews who fled to the Rhine Valley were, over the centuries, to spread across Europe. Ashkenazi Jewish communities of France, Italy and Germany, which were so numerous in the early Middle Ages, were pushed further and further eastwards due to persecutions from

the time of the Crusades, which began early in the 11th century. Many Jews fled to Eastern Europe, especially Poland. They spoke Yiddish, which is a combination of Middle High German and Hebrew, written in Hebrew script. Their non-Jewish neighbours ate abundant shellfish and pork, cooked with lard, and mixed milk with meat freely, none of which was permitted for Jews, so the only answer for them was to keep themselves apart. In Czarist Russia,

ABOVE: *An illumination from a Hebrew manuscript showing a synagogue (c.1350).*

they were only allowed to live in the Pale of Settlement, a portion of land that stretched from the Baltic Sea to the Black Sea. The Ashkenazi Jews lived – often uneasily – in *shtetlach* (villages) and never knew when they would be forced to flee again.

For the Jews who settled in Germany and Austria, the age of enlightenment was the Haskalah

(18th–19th century), when the reform movement freed them from the more restrictive bonds of religious adherence and allowed them to enter the secular world of arts, philosophy, science and music. German Jews amassed great knowledge and created a culture of depth and finesse. They became so intertwined with the culture of Germany that when the Holocaust was upon them they could not fathom how it could have happened, because they considered themselves German first and foremost.

Ashkenazi food was the food of a cold climate. Vegetables were pickled in salt and fermented, for instance cabbage became sauerkraut, which was stored to last the winter. Cucumbers were transformed into pickles, piquant treats to enliven the bland fare of winter. Fermented beetroot (beets) became russel, the basis for a traditional borscht. Fish – freshwater, rather than the sea fish enjoyed by the Sephardi Jews – were smoked and salted, as were meats. Because there was often insufficient kosher meat to go round, very small amounts would be bulked out with other ingredients and served as dumplings and pastries, or in casseroles and stews.

Grains and beans were eaten in abundance: healthy, hearty and filling, they were also *pareve*, so they could be mixed with either meat or milk. Often, but most usually for Shabbat or a festival, beans were cooked with meats in a dish known as cholent, which could be eaten when the family returned home from the synagogue.

ABOVE: *A group of Ashkenazi Jews sit outside their home in Jerusalem (1885).*

Ashkenazi food was often cooked in chicken or goose fat, enriched with golden onions. It was sometimes flavoured with honey, or a mixture of honey and piquant vinegar, to make a tangy sweet and sour sauce.

When potatoes were introduced from the New World, the Ashkenazi Jews adored them and incorporated them into their cuisine with great enthusiasm. Latkes and kugels, soups and dumplings were all prepared from this new and filling vegetable.

JEWS IN BRITAIN

The history of the Jews in Britain is long and complex. They first arrived in 1066 and were expelled by Edward I in 1290, a hundred years after the massacre at Clifford Tower of York's entire Jewish community. In 1655, after negotiations had been held between Manashe ben Israel and Oliver Cromwell, Jews were allowed to return and live in England.

Sephardi Jews then came to settle in England. They came via Holland, bringing with them the flavours and specialities of their native Portugal, which included their favourite dish, battered or crumbed fried fish. This was very likely the origin of Britain's traditional fish and chips, as the fish was subsequently combined with fried potatoes and eaten by the hungry masses – mostly Jews, often young women who worked in sweat shops in London's East End.

Today, most of Britain's Jewish communities live in London with smaller communities scattered around the rest of the country.

INFLUENCING THE FRENCH CUISINE

The French cuisine shows a strong influence from the Jewish community that settled there. Foie gras, often considered to be French, originated in ancient Egypt and was introduced to France by Jewish immigrants.

A JEWISH HERITAGE IN ITALY

The Italian Jewish community (Italkim), which is now very small as a result of the Holocaust and post-World War II emigration, was once grand, influential and active. The Italian cuisine has been influenced by these settlers. To this day, *carciofi alla Giudia* (artichokes in the Jewish manner) is a speciality of the ghetto of Rome, ghetto being a word that originated in Italy to describe an area set aside for Jews.

THE UNITED STATES AND THE DELI

In the early part of the 20th century there was a wave of immigration to the United States, which influenced the American table a great deal. The most obvious influence was the emergence of the delicatessen – or deli. In places that were home to Jewish communities from Eastern Europe, such as Chicago and Old New York, delis were places where hungry men with no homes of their own could go for a good meal. These men had usually travelled ahead of their wives and children to establish a new life. Lodging in rented rooms and working hard to save enough money to pay for their families to join them, they needed somewhere to eat that was kosher, and that gave them a taste of the land they left behind.

MODERN TIMES

The 20th century saw the end of many of the great Jewish communities – some as old as 2,500 years – and the start of others. Ashkenazim emigrating from Germany, Central Europe and Russia towards the end of the 19th century and the start of the 20th century often packed little by way of possessions, but they did take the traditions of the cuisine that we think of as Jewish: chicken soup and matzo balls, Viennese pastries, rye bread and bagels. The same dishes – familiarly called the food of the Old Country –

RIGHT: Twentieth-century Jewish immigrants await entry into New York.

travelled to Great Britain, Israel, Latin America and the United States with the refugees before, during and after World War II.

In many places, communities have regrouped. In Los Angeles you will find the Jewish community of Iran, which had been in Persia since 600BCE (BC) and held to their customs and cuisine. In Brooklyn there is a Cochinese synagogue, where Indian Jews cook their spicy delicacies for feasts.

Whether the traditional Jewish table is Sephardi, Ashkenazi, Conservative, Reform (Progressive), Orthodox or Chassidic is not what matters most. The most important factor is that the food it holds reflects both a people's lives and its culture. It is food for enjoying and for bringing families closer together, for giving reassurance in an ever-changing world and for sharing with old and new friends alike.

Holidays and festivals

The Jewish calendar is punctuated by holidays, festivals and observances, shared by the entire community. Personal milestones in the lives of individuals such as Bar or Bat Mitzvahs, weddings and the birth of babies are also celebrated. Each festival has a special significance, and is accompanied by its own songs, stories, admonitions, activities, prayers and, of course, foods.

The Jewish year follows the 354–5 day lunar calendar, as opposed to the 365–6 day solar year, so while each Jewish festival falls on precisely the same date in each year of the Jewish calendar, the dates will differ on a Gregorian calendar. For synchronicity, and also to keep the months in their appropriate season, a 13th month is added to the Jewish calendar every two or three years. In the northern hemisphere, therefore, Rosh Hashanah will always be celebrated between summer and autumn, while Chanukkah always heralds winter and Pesach ushers in the spring.

Jewish holidays always begin at sundown on the day before. The year of celebrations starts around September, with Rosh Hashanah, the Jewish New Year, and progresses through Yom Kippur, the Day of

Atonement, which is nine days later. Sukkot, the harvest festival of thanksgiving, follows, ending with Simchat Torah, the festival of the Torah. Around December comes Chanukkah, the festival of lights. Tu b'Shevat, the Holiday of the Trees, comes next, around February, and this in turn is followed by Purim, a festival that could be considered a kind of Jewish Mardi Gras or carnival. Pesach commemorates Israel's deliverance from Egypt. During the eight-day festival, Jews consume particular foods and drinks, eschewing those that contain leaven. Shavuot celebrates the Giving of the Torah, while Tish b'Av is a day of fasting, when the Destruction of the Temple is mourned.

Many Jewish communities also observe Yom Hatsmaut, Israeli Independence Day, which is celebrated on 14 May. Yom Ha Shoah, the

ABOVE: *Jewish holidays commemorate the past and demand tradition and ritual.*

Holocaust Remembrance Day, is observed shortly after Pesach, honouring the millions who died.

The most important festival and observance of them all is the Sabbath or Shabbat, which comes not once a year, but once a week.

SHABBAT

This is the Sabbath, the day of rest. It is the weekly oasis of peace in the sea of hectic life. Even those who are not observant in other ways will often enjoy keeping Shabbat. It is a day for refraining from work, escaping the chaos of the working week, focusing on the spiritual, and enjoying family life. The word *shabbat* means cessation of labour, and it is a time to relax with family and friends.

The origins of Shabbat are related in Genesis, the first book of the Bible, which describes how God created the world in six days and rested on the seventh. In the fourth commandment of the Ten Commandments, it is also decreed that Shabbat is a day of rest that must be kept holy (Exodus 31:17).

Observant Jews do not do any work, handle money, carry loads, light fires, tear paper, watch television or listen to the radio. They also may not cook, which has led to ingenious ways of providing freshly cooked food without infringing the rule.

On the eve of Shabbat a festive meal is served. It begins with the lighting and blessing of the candles before sundown. Further blessings are then said over the challah, and the Kiddush (sanctifying blessing) is said over the wine.

The meal on Friday night includes chicken soup, and a chicken or braised meat. Guests will be invited, and the table set with white linen, flowers and the finest china. The next day's meal will be simmered in a low oven, as no cooking is allowed on the Sabbath.

ROSH HASHANAH

The Jewish year begins in September or October with Rosh Hashanah, which means the head of the year. This is the start of the Ten Days of Penitence, also called the Days of Awe, which end with Yom Kippur. Jews are encouraged to spend these days in retrospection, considering their behaviour and how to make amends, improving their own lives and the lives of those around them.

The holidays of Rosh Hashanah and Yom Kippur are often referred to as the High Holy Days, and many Jews consider them so important that even if they observe no other festivals in the year, at this time they will go to synagogue, partake of a festive meal, and recite the prayers and blessings.

A ceremonial *shofar* (ram's horn) is blown on Rosh Hashanah, as it is on Yom Kippur. The haunting sounds of the *shofar* reminds Jews of their long history and of the ancient convenant between the people of Israel and God.

Rosh Hashanah begins, as usual, at sundown on the evening before. Candles are lit, the bread is blessed, and the Kiddush is recited over the wine. A festive meal is prepared. This includes sweet foods such as apples dipped in honey, bringing the promise of sweetness in the year ahead. The challah, which is shaped into a round, rather than the more familiar oval

ABOVE: *Shabbat begins with the blessings being said over a loaf of challah and a cup of wine.*

plait, is studded with raisins or small sweets (candies). Honey replaces salt for the blessing of the challah.

YOM KIPPUR

The 10th day of Tishri, the first month in the Jewish calendar, is Yom Kippur – the Day of Atonement. It is the most solemn day of the year and marks God's forgiveness of the Israelites after they worshipped the golden calf while Moses received the tablets of the law from God on Mount Sinai.

The meal on the eve of Yom Kippur is eaten in the afternoon, before sunset. Chicken soup is the preferred food, as it is for almost every festive occasion. For Ashkenazi Jews it is traditional to eat the soup with knaidlach (matzo balls) or kreplach filled with chicken, while for Sephardi Jews there are many variations.

BELOW: *The ceremonial* shofar *(ram's horn) is blown at Rosh Hashanah to welcome in the New Year.*

All foods eaten at this time must be simple and not too salty or spicy as it is difficult to fast with a raging thirst. It is intended that penitents should feel a few hunger pangs while they are fasting, but they should not get into any difficulty during this period.

Families and friends gather together for celebrations to break the fast after Yom Kippur. It is a happy occasion after the solemnity of the day's observance. Sephardim serve eggs, the symbol of life, and almost all Jews enjoy sweet foods such as honey cake and fruit.

Dishes are prepared the day before Yom Kippur so that they are ready for the end of the fast. For Ashkenazi Jews, it is a good time to eat bagels, cream cheese, lox (smoked salmon), kugels and herring. A break-the-fast party is much like a brunch, but with a feeling of lightness of soul and a spirit of looking forward to the new year.

SUKKOT

This festival is observed by building a *sukkah*, which is a temporary three-sided hut. If the weather permits, meals during the seven-day festival are eaten in the *sukkah*. Four plants – Arba Minim – decorate the *sukkah*. They are: the etrog (a lemon-like citron); the lulav (palm branch); the arava (willow branch); and the myrtle. Each of these has a deep significance. The etrog is shaped like a heart and symbolizes the hope of divine forgiveness for the desires of our heart; the lulav symbolizes Israel's loyalty to God; while the myrtle is shaped like an eye and represents the

ABOVE: *Children spin the dreidel as part of the Chanukkah celebrations.*

hope that greed and envy will be forgiven. The arava is shaped like a mouth and represents forgiveness for idle talk and lies.

Since Sukkot is a harvest festival, fruit and vegetables are eaten. Cabbage is stuffed to make holishkes, and strudel is made from apple. Pomegranates and persimmons are considered a Sukkot treat.

The eighth day of Sukkot is Shemeni Atzeret, when memorial prayers are said. The next day, Simchat Torah, is the festival of rejoicing in the Torah, when the weekly readings of the Torah in the synagogue finish and the cycle begins again. Children are often brought to the synagogue to celebrate Simchat Torah.

CHANUKKAH

Throughout the world, beginning on the eve of the 25th of Kislev, which falls in November or December, Jews celebrate Chanukkah, the festival of

lights, by lighting an oil lamp or menorah filled with candles, lighting one every night for eight nights until all are lit.

The festival commemorates the Maccabean victory over Antiochus IV in the year 165BCE (BC). When the Jewish Maccabees returned to the Temple, after defeating the Syrians, they found it pillaged, and the eternal light extinguished. They lit the lamp, but there was only enough oil for one day. However a miracle occurred and the holy lamp continued to burn for eight days until a messenger returned with a new supply of oil.

At Chanukkah, Jews eat foods cooked in oil, to remind them of the lamp that burned and burned. Chanukkah is a happy and joyous celebration. The Shulhkan Arukh – the code of law – forbids mourning and fasting during this time, encouraging great merry-making.

PURIM

This festival is one of celebration, feasting and drinking. It falls on the 14th Adar, around February or March, and reminds Jews of the triumph of freedom and goodness over evil. Special foods are eaten at Purim.

In Ashkenazi cultures, triangular pastries filled with nuts or dried fruit are served. The filling is meant to commemorate Esther, who ate only fruits and nuts in the palace, as the kitchen was not kosher. For North African Sephardim, fried pastries drenched in honey and sprinkled with nuts, called oznei Haman (the ears of Haman), are a favourite Purim treat.

PESACH

The Passover festival, Pesach, is one of the biggest festivals in the Jewish year. It commemorates the story of the exodus of the Hebrew slaves from Egypt, a flight that turned a tribe of slaves into a cohesive people. During this festival, Jews celebrate the flight for freedom of all humanity – the freedom of spirit as well as personal, religious and physical freedom.

Pesach falls sometime around March or April. The word pesach means passing over, and represents the passing of the houses whose doorways the Israelites had splashed with lamb's blood, so that those inside remained unharmed when the angel of death ravaged Egypt, slaying the first-born sons.

For eight days no leavened foods are permitted, ruling out breads made with yeast. Crisp flat breads called matzos are served, as a reminder of the Israelites who in their escape to the desert, only had time to make flatbreads, cooked on hot stones.

BELOW: *A ritual Seder plate.*

On the first night of the festival a ritual meal called the Seder is served. The meal revolves around the reading of the Haggadah, the story of the exodus from Egypt and from slavery.

SEFIRAH

Between Pesach and the next major festival, Shavuot, is a period called Sefirah. It is a solemn time of observance rather than a festival. Beginning at the end of Pesach, it commemorates the day when a sheaf of young barley – the Omer – was traditionally brought into the Temple in Jerusalem.

Observing this period is called Counting the Omer. During this time, the Observant do not celebrate weddings, have other celebrations or even cut their hair.

LAG B'OMER

This happy day falls on the 33rd day of counting and is the one break in the solemn time of Sefirah. Lag b'Omer is a day made for celebrating out of doors and picnicking. For Observant Jews, Lag b'Omer is the day in spring when you could schedule a wedding or have a haircut.

TU B'SHEVAT

This festival is known as the Holiday of the Trees. It is one of the four holidays that celebrate nature, as mentioned in the Mishnah (part of the

ABOVE: *Prayers for Shavuot.*

Talmud). Tu b'Shevat occurs in February, when the sap begins to rise in the fruit trees of Israel. To celebrate, it is customary to eat different kinds of fruits and nuts.

SHAVUOT

The word *shavuot* means weeks in Hebrew, as this festival comes seven weeks after Pesach. In English it is known as Pentecost, which comes from the Greek, meaning 50 days. It is also sometimes referred to as the Festival of the Torah, as it tells the story of the Israelites wandering through the desert and commemorates the giving of the Jewish scriptures, the Torah, and the Ten Commandments to Moses. This festival is also the Feast of the First Fruits, one of the ancient pilgrimages to Jerusalem, when the first fruits and grains of the season were brought as offerings.

The laws
of **Kashrut**

Kashrut is the set of ritual dietary laws that are set out in the Talmud. Food that conforms to those standards is described as kosher. Whether a Jew comes from a land where onions, garlic and chicken fat are freely eaten, or one whose cuisine includes hot peppers, spices and olive oil, the meals eaten in the Observant Jewish household will not taste the same as food prepared from similar ingredients by non-Jewish neighbours, because the former will conform to the rules of Kashrut.

BELOW: *Beef, goat and lamb, when prepared appropriately, are all permitted by the laws of Kashrut.*

Though the basic principles of Kashrut are outlined in the Bible, they have been ruled upon and commented upon by rabbis in the Shulhan Aruckh, the code of Jewish law. There is no reason given for the laws of Kashrut, though many have suggested that hygiene, food safety and health might be contributory factors. The rabbis state, however, that no reason or rationale is needed; obeying the laws of Kashrut is a commandment from God.

PERMITTED MEATS
Only certain types of meat are allowed, based on the text in Leviticus 11:3, which states: "Whatsoever parteth the hoof, and is clovenfooted, and cheweth the cud...that shall ye eat". These conditions mean that ox, sheep, goat, hart, gazelle, roebuck, antelope and mountain sheep may be eaten. No birds or animals of prey are allowed, nor are scavengers, creeping insects or reptiles.

PERMITTED BIRDS
The Torah is not quite so clear when it comes to identifying which birds may be eaten. Instead, it lists 24 species of forbidden fowl. In general, chickens, ducks, turkeys and geese are allowed, but this can vary. Goose is popular among Ashkenazim, while Yemenite Jews consider it to be of both the land and sea and therefore forbidden.

RITUAL SLAUGHTER
For kosher animals to become kosher meat, they must be slaughtered ritually by *shechita*. An animal that dies of natural causes, or is killed by another animal, is forbidden. The knife for slaughter must be twice as long as the animal's throat and extremely sharp and smooth.

The *shochet* (ritual slaughterer) must expertly sever the animal's trachea and oesophagus without grazing its spine; any delay would bring terror to the animal and render the meat unkosher.

KASHERING MEAT
This is the term used to describe the removal of blood from an animal immediately after slaughter, which is essential if the meat is to be labelled kosher.

To Jews, blood is a symbol of life, and the prohibition against consuming it comes from the

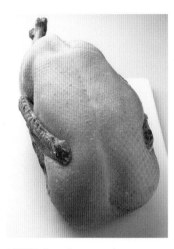

ABOVE: *Goose is very popular among Eastern European Jews who, in the past, often raised them for their fat livers and to serve at holiday meals.*

scriptures: "Therefore I said unto the children of Israel, No soul of you shall eat blood…" (Leviticus 17:12).

All meat must be kashered by soaking, salting or grilling (broiling) so that no blood remains.

PERMITTED FISH

To be considered kosher, all fish must have detachable scales and fins. Other sea creatures that are forbidden include all shellfish and crustaceans, sea urchin, octopus and squid.

DAIRY PRODUCTS

Deuteronomy states "Thou shalt not seethe a kid in his mother's milk." This is the basis for the rule that dairy foods and meat must not be cooked together. After eating a meat meal, a certain amount of time must elapse before dairy food

can be consumed. Some communities wait six hours, while others wait only two hours.

To ensure the complete separation of meat and milk, kosher kitchens have separate dishes, pans and washing-up utensils for each. These must be stored separately.

CHEESE AND RENNET

Natural rennet, the ingredient used to curdle milk for cheese-making, comes from the lining of an animal's stomach. Therefore, the cheese made from it is not kosher. Much modern cheese is made with vegetable rennet, but not necessarily labelled as such, so to be sure, eat only cheeses that are marked "Suitable for Vegetarians".

GELATINE

Because gelatine is made from animal bones, it is not kosher. Kosher gelatine made from seaweed (carrageen) is vegetarian, and must be used instead.

BELOW: Pareve *foods such as barley, onions, aubergines (eggplant), tomatoes and eggs can be eaten with either meat or dairy foods.*

PAREVE FOODS

In Yiddish, these foods are known as *pareve* and in Hebrew they are *parva*. These are the neutral foods that are neither meat nor dairy. They do not have the same restrictions imposed upon them and can be eaten with meat or dairy foods. All plant foods such as vegetables, grains and fruit are *pareve*, as are eggs and permitted fish. Jews who keep kosher will not eat *pareve* foods that have been prepared outside the home as they could have been prepared using non-kosher fats.

Kashrut certification

To be sure that any packaged food is kosher, look for a symbol of recognized certification every time you buy, as additives and methods can change. There are numerous certifying boards, and many Jews will eat only packaged foods certified by specific boards. If a food is certified as Glatt Kosher it conforms to a particularly stringent Kashrut, which requires, among other things, that the lungs be more thoroughly examined.

Some Observant Jews will eat foods such as canned tomatoes, for the only ingredients are tomatoes and salt. Others avoid such foods, as they could have been contaminated on the production line. Very strict Jews extend their watchfulness even to the basics, and will eat only sugar with the rabbinical supervision marking, to be sure it has not been tainted by other unkosher food products or insects.

Dairy

In both the Ashkenazi and Sephardi kitchen, all dairy foods are held in very high esteem, a tribute to the biblical description of the land of Israel as a "land of milk and honey".

There are strict rules concerning the consumption of dairy foods, but they do not have great religious significance except during the festival of Shavuot. This is sometimes known as the dairy festival and is a time when dairy products are enjoyed for main meals, in preference to meat, which is normally enjoyed at festivals and celebrations.

MILK AND DAIRY PRODUCTS

The milk taken from any kosher animal is considered kosher. Cows, goats and sheep are all milked and the milk is then drunk or made into various dairy products such as butter, yogurt and sour cream. The influences of the past can be seen in the dairy products that are still enjoyed by Jews today.

In the past, in Northern Europe, milk from cows was readily available and, because the weather was cool, spoilage was not a great problem. Many towns and villages had small dairies that produced sour cream, butter, buttermilk, cottage cheese and cream cheese, and families often owned a cow or two of their own.

In Lithuania, however, goats tended to be kept more often than cows and were referred to as Jewish cattle. In warmer countries, especially those situated around the Mediterranean, goats and sheep were much easier to raise, and their milk was more suitable for making fermented dairy products such as yogurt, feta cheese and halloumi. Today, Israel is a great producer of many different types of yogurts and sour creams.

Cheeses

A wide variety of kosher cheeses are produced in modern-day Israel, including kashkaval, which resembles a mild Cheddar; halloumi; Bin-Gedi, which is similar to Camembert, and Galil, which is modelled on Roquefort. Fresh goat's cheeses are also particularly popular in Israel and are of a very good quality.

Cream cheese has been very popular with Ashkenazim since the days of *shtetlach*, where it was made in small, Jewish-owned dairies, and sold in earthenware pots or wrapped in leaves.

Soft cheeses such as cream cheese and cottage cheese were also often made in the home. Cream cheese is the classic spread for bagels, when it is known as a schmear. It can also be flavoured with other ingredients such as chopped spring onions (scallions) and smoked salmon and is widely available in supermarkets and delis.

ABOVE (CLOCKWISE FROM TOP LEFT): *Cottage cheese, cream cheese, feta and kashkaval are among the many kosher Jewish cheeses.*

Dairy delis

These were a great legacy of New York's Lower East Side Jewish community. Among the most famous of the dairy deli restaurants was Ratners, known for its elderly waiters who were invariably grumpy, nosy, bossy and ultimately endearing.

Dairy shops and restaurants sold specialities such as cheese-filled blintzes, cheesecake, cream cheese shmears and knishes.

Among other treats on offer at most dairy delis were boiled potatoes with sour cream, hot or cold borscht, cheese kugels and noodles with cottage cheese.

Eggs

These represent the mysteries of life and death and are very important in Jewish cuisine. They are brought to a family on the birth of a child, and served after a funeral to remind the mourners that, in the midst of death, we are still embraced by life. They also represent fertility.

In some Sephardi communities, an egg will be included as part of a bride's costume, or the young couple will be advised to step over fish roe or eat double-yolked eggs to help increase their fertility.

Eggs are *pareve* (see page 197) so may be eaten with either meat or dairy foods. They are very nutritious and filling and provide a good source of protein when other sources may be lacking or forbidden due to the strict laws of Kashrut (see pages 196–7).

EGGS FOR PESACH

These feature prominently in the Pesach Seder festival – both symbolically and as a food. It is said that a whole egg represents the strength of being a whole people (unbroken, the shell is strong; broken, it is weak).

Eggs are also an important ingredient during the festival of Pesach, as yeast, the usual traditional raising agent, may not be used for baking. Eggs, when beaten into a cake mixture (batter), can help the cake to rise.

Making roasted eggs

A roasted egg is traditionally placed on the Seder plate to represent the cycle of life. It is symbolic of the ritual sacrifice made at the Temple during biblical times, and is not usually eaten.

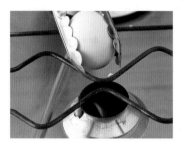

A hard-boiled egg is roasted over a medium gas flame, or in the oven.

Making eggs in salt water

This simple dish is the first thing eaten when the Pesach service is over. It is only eaten at this time.

1 Hard-boil the eggs. Meanwhile, in a small bowl, dissolve 2.5ml/½ tsp salt in 120ml/4fl oz/½ cup warm water. Cool, then chill.

2 Shell the eggs and serve with the salt water for dipping, or place them in the bowl of salt water.

HAMINADOS EGGS

These are a Sephardi speciality. Whole eggs are cooked slowly with onion skins or coffee grounds, to colour the shells. Alternatively, they may be added to the slow-cooked stew, dafina. They are delicious mashed with leftover cholent, in savoury pastries, or chopped and added to simmered brown broad (fava) beans with a little garlic, onion, olive oil and hot chilli sauce.

Making haminados eggs

Cooking the eggs with onion skins colours the egg shells but does not impart any flavour to the egg inside.

1 Place 12 eggs in a pan and add salt and pepper. Drop in the brown outer skins from 8–10 onions, pour over water to cover and 90ml/6 tbsp oil.

2 Bring to the boil, then lower the heat to low and cook for 6 hours, adding more water, if required. Shell and serve.

Classic deli dishes

Hard-boiled egg, chopped with onion and mixed with a little chicken fat or mayonnaise, is one of the oldest Jewish dishes. In modern-day Israel, an avocado is often mashed with the eggs. Scrambled eggs with browned onion and shredded smoked chicken on slices of rye toast or bagels make a perfect brunch.

Meat

For Observant Jews, meat must be kosher. Originally, any Jew versed in the ritual could slaughter meat, but this changed in the 13th century, with the appointment of shochets (ritual slaughterers). To qualify for this post, a man needed to be very learned, pious and upstanding.

Meat has always been an expensive but highly prized item on the Jewish table. For Ashkenazim, it was made even more costly with the levying of a hefty government tax (*korobka*). This, together with a community tax for Jewish charities, brought the price to twice that for non-kosher meat. None of this deterred Jews from eating meat, however; they simply saved it for special occasions.

BELOW: *Veal escalopes (US scallops) are often pounded to make the classic Viennese schnitzel.*

LAMB AND MUTTON

These were favoured by the Sephardim from North Africa and other Arabic lands until the early 20th century, when the strong French influence introduced beef and veal to their table. Due to the time-consuming removal of the sciatic nerve required by the laws of Kashrut, the Ashkenazim avoided eating the hindquarters of lamb and mutton until the 15th century, when a meat shortage made the lengthy procedure worthwhile.

BEEF

This is very popular, especially among European Jews. Brisket is grainy and rough textured, but yields a wonderful flavour when cooked for a long time. The same applies to the short ribs and the chuck or bola. Many of these cuts are not only excellent for pot-roasting and soups; they also make good salt or corned beef and pastrami. Beef shin makes a marvellous soup.

Sausages and salami

Both Askenazim and Sephardim use beef to make a wide array of sausages and salamis. The Ashkenazim tend to favour cured sausages such as frankfurters, knockwurst, knobblewurst and spicy dried sausages, while the Sephardim favour fresh sausages, such as the spicy merguez from North Africa and France.

VEAL

This is a favourite meat for all Jewish communities, because it is so delicate and light: shoulder roast, breast of veal, shank and rib chops are all very popular cuts along with minced (ground) veal. The breast would often be stuffed, then braised with mixed vegetables; minced veal was made into cutlets and meatballs; and, in Vienna, slices of shoulder, or escalopes (US scallops), were pounded until they were very thin, then coated in breadcrumbs and fried to make the famous crisp, golden schnitzel.

Meatballs in many guises

Spiced or seasoned meatballs are very popular throughout the Jewish world and come in many different forms.
• Russian bitkis are made from minced (ground) beef, often with chopped onion, and may be fried, grilled (broiled) or simmered, often alongside a chicken for a Shabbat or other festive meal.
• Kotleta are flattened meatballs that are fried.
• Cylindrical Romanian mitetetlai are flavoured with garlic, often with parsley, and are fried or grilled (broiled) until brown.
• The Sephardi world has myriad meatballs: albondigas, boulettes, kefta or kofta, and yullikas. They are highly spiced and can be grilled (broiled), cooked over an open fire or simmered in sauces.

OTHER MEATS

These include goat and deer (venison). Goat is popular in Sephardi cooking and is often used in dishes where lamb could be used, such as spicy stews, curries and meatballs. Venison is cooked in similar ways to beef.

OFFAL

Historically, poorer families tended to eat cheaper cuts of meat, such as feet, spleen, lungs, intestines, liver, tongue and brains. These were popular with both Ashkenazim and Sephardim, especially Yemenite Jews, who are still famed today for their delicious spicy offal soups.

COOKING KOSHER MEAT

Kosher meat is usually tough because the cuts eaten tend to contain a high proportion of muscle; the meat is not tenderized by being hung but must be butchered within 72 hours of slaughter; and because the salting of meat to remove blood produces a dry result. Because of this, meat is generally cooked very slowly by stewing, braising, pot-roasting and simmering until the meat is tender.

These long, slow methods are also ideal for the Shabbat meal, which can be prepared and cooked ahead of time, then left in the oven to grow beautifully tender.

When meat is cooked quickly, for instance in kebabs, the meat is marinated first to tenderize it. Chopping or mincing (grinding) meat has a similar effect, which is why so many Jewish meat recipes are for meatballs, patties and meat loaves. These dishes also allow a modest amount of meat to be stretched.

TRADITIONAL FLAVOURINGS

Each region favours certain flavourings. The Polish choose sweet-and-sour flavours; the Germans sweet and fruity ones; the Russians savoury, with onions; the Lithuanians spicy and peppery. Sephardim favour spices and fresh seasonal vegetables. Moroccans add sweet, fruity flavours to their meat; Tunisians prefer sharp spices; Turkish Jews add tomatoes and fresh herbs such as dill; while the Persians prefer delicate flavours, with fresh herbs, fruits and vegetables and also beans.

Making meatloaf

A traditional Ashkenazi dish, meatloaf is called klops. It is delicious served either hot or cold.

1 Preheat the oven to 180°C/ 350°F/Gas 4. Combine 800g/1³/₄lb minced (ground) meat, 2 grated onions, 5 chopped garlic cloves, 1 grated carrot, chopped parsley, 60ml/4 tbsp breadcrumbs, 45ml/ 3tbsp ketchup and 1 beaten egg.

2 Form into a loaf and place in a roasting pan. Spread over 60ml/ 4 tbsp tomato ketchup and arrange 2 sliced tomatoes on top. Sprinkle over 2–3 sliced onions.

3 Cover the pan with foil and bake for 1 hour. Remove the foil, increase the temperature to 200°C/400°F/Gas 6 and remove some of the onions. Bake for 15 minutes, or until the meat is cooked and the onions browned.

Meats from the deli counter

Traditionally, Jewish delis sold either meat or dairy foods. Meat delis always have a wonderful choice of cured meats and sausages – salt beef on rye, salami, smoky pastrami or frankfurters and knockwurst with sauerkraut.

ABOVE: *Beef salami, salt beef and spicy pastrami are classic deli fare.*

Poultry

This is considered meat in the laws of Kashrut, and is therefore subject to all the same rules as regards slaughter and preparation. Any part of a permitted bird can be eaten.

CHICKEN

This is probably the most popular fowl for both Sephardim and Ashkenazim. Like beef and lamb, chicken was once reserved for the Shabbat or other festive meal. However, chicken was later served more frequently as people often raised a few chickens of their own at home and could take them to the shochet when the right time came.

Chicken is often first simmered in water or stock to make soup, then roasted for a main course.

Meatballs made from minced (ground) chicken were a favourite food of Persian and Turkish Jews, especially when simmered along with aubergine (eggplant). Iraqis were famous for their spiced chicken croquettes, which they introduced to India and Burma. Indian Jews cook marvellous chicken curries, substituting coconut milk for yogurt, which is not permitted with chicken.

A favourite Sephardi dish, eaten on the streets of Jerusalem, consists of chicken giblets and livers, grilled (broiled) until they are brown and crisp, and then eaten immediately with freshly cooked pitta bread and a very hot, spicy pepper sauce.

ABOVE: *Chicken is used in an array of classic Jewish dishes.*

OTHER BIRDS

Turkey, duck, goose and farmed pigeon (US squab), quail and poussin are also eaten. In Morocco, it is traditional for bridal couples to be served pigeons cooked with sweet fruits on their wedding night, to grant them a sweet life together.

In the Sephardi tradition, birds were often stuffed with couscous, spicy meat, rice and dried fruit, or with herbs and milder spices such as cinnamon. The Sephardim also liked stewed poultry with quinces or pomegranates, or flavoured with tomatoes, (bell) peppers, chickpeas or olives. The art of raising geese for foie gras was acquired by Jews in Ancient Egypt, and it is believed that it was they who introduced the delicacy to France.

SCHMALTZ AND GREBENES

Rendered chicken fat (schmaltz), and the crisp morsels of skin left over after rendering (grebenes), are widely used in Jewish cooking. Schmaltz was long considered a symbol of abundance and there is a traditional Yiddish saying, " "He's so lucky that even when he falls, he falls right into a schmaltz!" Spread schmaltz on bread with onions or use it to flavour cholent or to make chopped liver.

Making schmaltz and grebenes

One chicken won't make very much schmaltz, so save the fat and skin from several chickens and chill in the refrigerator or freeze until you have 450g/1lb.

1 Cut the fat and skin into small pieces. Place in a large, heavy pan and pour over water to cover. Bring to the boil and cook over a high heat until the water has evaporated.

2 Lower the heat and add about 2½ chopped onions and 1–2 garlic cloves.

3 Cook over a medium heat, removing the garlic when golden.

4 When all the chicken fat has been rendered and the grebenes are crunchy, remove the grebenes carefully with a slotted spoon.

Fish

Permitted types of fish are classified as **pareve,** *so there are no restrictions with regard to combining them with other ingredients. Its versatility makes fish extremely important on the Jewish dinner table. It may hold centre stage, as when a whole fish is served at Rosh Hashanah, but more often it is served as an appetizer or as one of several dishes as part of a buffet.*

From the fresh fish counter, there is always a wide choice on offer. Sea bass, cod, sole and flounder, haddock, hake and mackerel are all popular sea fish, with perch, pike and trout among the best-loved of the freshwater varieties.

Some fish are thought of as being more Jewish than others. However, this apparent preference for certain fish has simply come about because of geography and traditional availability.

For example, carp is a particular favourite among Ashkenazi Jews, as is pike. Carp was brought to Europe by Jews who encountered it in China when they were involved in the silk trade in the 15th century, while pike was introduced into the USA from Germany in the 19th century and grew in popularity as waves of Jewish immigrants arrived in the country from all over the world.

Making jellied carp

This traditional, and delicious, dish of poached carp in jelly is a legacy of the Jews of Eastern Europe.

1 Cut 1kg/2^1/4lb prepared fresh carp into 8–10 slices. Heat 15ml/1 tbsp oil in a large pan. Add 2^1/2 chopped onions and sauté until golden brown.

2 Add 2–3 bay leaves, 1–2 parsley and thyme sprigs, 1–2 lemon slices and the carp to the pan and season well.

3 Pour 450ml/^{3}/4 pint/2 cups hot fish stock and 250ml/8fl oz/1 cup white wine into the pan. Bring to the boil, then simmer for 1 hour until the fish is tender. Cool slightly, then remove the carp and pack it into a mould.

4 Strain the fish stock through a fine sieve (strainer) into a large bowl.

5 Dissolve 2 sachets of kosher gelatine in 150ml/^{1}/4 pint/^{2}/3 cup of the stock, then stir into the remaining stock. Pour the mixture over the fish and chill in the refrigerator until firm.

6 Serve the jellied carp with lemon wedges and horseradish.

Fish from the deli counter

No Ashkenazi celebration is complete without some kind of fish from the deli counter. A good deli will smell deliciously of smoked and cured fish.

The art of preserving fish is a speciality of the Ashkenazi Jews. They perfected the technique so that stocks of fish would last all year. Methods used included salting, brining, smoking and marinating.

In a good deli you will find silky smoked salmon (lox), its natural orange colour providing a contrast to the smoked whitefish in its shimmering gold skin. In addition there will be salt herring, smoked herring, pickled herring, herring in sour cream, herring in brine and herring salad. You will find also gefilte fish in the deli, either freshly made or ready-made in jars, the liquid jellied and flavoured sweetly in the Polish manner, or spicy and peppery, in the typical Russian or Lithuanian tradition.

BELOW: *Spicy, piquant pickled herring rollmops and thinly sliced smoked salmon are perfect for a Shabbat brunch.*

Grains

For Jews, grains, beans, peas and lentils have long been the staff of life and have fuelled generations.

In many places, a certain type of grain or pulse (legume) actually helped to define the cuisine of the community. In Romania it was mamaliga, a cornmeal porridge that resembles polenta; in North Africa it was couscous; and for many places in the East, the staple food was rice. In Russia, Poland and the Ukraine, kasha (buckwheat) was widely eaten. Pulses are added to cholent, hamim and dafina, the slow-cooked stews that are traditionally served for Shabbat.

KASHA

This nutty, earthy grain is the partially milled grain or groat of buckwheat. It is traditionally used in Ashkenazi cooking and is very evocative for Ashkenazim who grew up eating it. Kasha is traditionally served with roasts and pot-roasts, bathed in gravy and meat juices, or may be used as a filling for knishes and dumplings. It can also be combined with onions, wild mushrooms and noodles. Kasha varnishkes, a classic Ashkenazi dish of kasha, butterfly-shaped noodles and onions, is traditionally eaten at the festival of Purim.

Making kasha

The grains may be fine, medium or coarse. Kasha should be toasted before being cooked, to keep it from going mushy and give it a nutty flavour. It is often toasted with egg before being simmered, to keep the grains separate.

To toast kasha, heat in a heavy pan over a medium heat for a few minutes until the grains start to give off their aroma. Add stock, bring to the boil, reduce the heat and cover. Simmer gently for 10–20 minutes until tender.

To toast kasha with egg, combine about 250g/9oz/1¼ cups kasha in a bowl with 1 beaten egg. Add the mixture to a cold heavy pan. Stir well, then turn on the heat to medium-high. Stir constantly while the grains toast and the egg sets. When the grains look dry, add stock or water and cook the kasha as above.

LEFT (CLOCKWISE FROM TOP LEFT):
Pareve grains such as barley, kasha (buckwheat) and bulgur wheat are important staples in both the Ashkenazi and Sephardi kitchens.

MAMALIGA

This golden cornmeal is widely used in Eastern Europe and is Romania's national dish. It resembles polenta and can be eaten either soft and porridge-like, or spread out on a baking tray and left to chill in the refrigerator until firm, then sliced and fried or grilled (broiled). It is good eaten either hot or cold.

Mamaliga is eaten by everyone in Romania, whether they are Jewish or not. For breakfast, it is drizzled with honey or jam and served with sour cream; for lunch it is topped with cottage cheese or Brinza, a cheese similar to feta, and butter. It also tastes great with roasted (bell) peppers and tomatoes. Alternatively, for a meat meal, with a pot-roast and gravy, or grilled (broiled) beef patties or beef sausages.

BARLEY

This high-protein food is a good source of B vitamins. It is an indispensable ingredient in Eastern European dishes such as mushroom and barley soup, or barley with vegetables and butter (lima) beans. A small amount of meat is also sometimes added.

BULGUR WHEAT

This is the partially milled grain of the whole wheat and is widely used in cooking throughout the Middle East. It comes in different sizes, from small and fine through to large. Bulgur wheat is sometimes eaten in place of couscous or rice, with savoury stews or soups.

ABOVE (CLOCKWISE FROM TOP RIGHT):
Beans, split peas and lentils are rich in protein and can be added to stews to eke out a small amount of meat.

COUSCOUS

This grain-like staple actually consists of tiny pellets of pasta, though it is usually categorized as a grain. It has always been very popular with the Jews of North Africa and, when they came to Israel, they brought it with them, in various different sizes. It is easy to prepare and is usually steamed over a light and savoury spicy stew of vegetables, meats, fish or fruit. Many different types of couscous are available and they are cooked in different ways. Ordinary couscous is moistened with cold water and left to plump up. It is then steamed over a stew. Fast-cooking couscous only needs to be combined with boiling water, then heated through or left to soak.

Israeli couscous, a pea-sized toasted pasta, is cooked in the same way as pasta. It gives a succulent result and is very good in soups and fish dishes.

RICE

This is widely eaten by Jews throughout the world. Chelou is a classic dish of the Persian Jews. As it cooks, the rice at the base of the pan is allowed to form a crisp crust (*tahdeeg*), which is then stirred into the tender rice, providing a tasty contrast of textures. Sometimes, thinly sliced potatoes are also added.

Many Iranian Jewish specialities use chelou as their base, topping it with herby vegetable or meat stews. At Rosh Hashanah, Iranian Jews particularly favour rice. The many tiny grains of rice represent the many grains of happiness that are hoped for during the coming year.

CHICKPEAS

These are eaten in great quantities by Sephardi Jews, and Eastern European Jews serve them to celebrate a Brit Milah. They are milled into flour and used as a thickener by Indian and Middle Eastern Jews, and are soaked and ground to make falafel, which is considered by many to be Israel's national dish.

RIGHT: Israeli couscous (in front) has much larger grains than regular couscous (behind).

DRIED BEANS AND PEAS

Broad (fava) beans and black-eyed beans (peas) are very popular with the Sephardim. Broad beans are very ancient and have been found at pre-pottery Neolithic B levels in Jericho. Black-eyed beans originated in Ethiopia about four thousand years ago and were recorded in Judea about 1500BCE (BC). Both are eaten in soups and stews. Dried broad beans are cooked and eaten with garlic, olive oil, hard-boiled eggs and a little tahini.

LENTILS

All types of lentil are made into soup, from split red lentils, which cook relatively quickly, to the superior tasting brown variety. Yellow and green split peas are also popular. In Genesis, the story is told of how Esau sold his birthright for a pottage of lentils.

Vegetables

Many different types of vegetables have particular significance in celebrations to mark religious festivals. For instance, at Rosh Hashanah, pumpkin may be served, its golden colour signifying prosperity. Green vegetables will be on the table, symbolizing renewal and happiness, while dried beans and peas signify abundance.

Carrots for Rosh Hashanah are cooked in honey to signify a sweet new year. In contrast, at the Pesach Seder, bitter herbs are eaten as a reminder of the bitterness of slavery. At the same time, Ashkenazim eat broad (fava) beans, since this was

ABOVE: *Root vegetables such as carrots, turnips and beetroot (beets) are typical Ashkenazi staples.*

what the Israelite slaves were fed during their captivity in Egypt. When Ashkenazim celebrate Chanukkah, they do so with potato latkes.

Seven different types of vegetable are used by North African Jews to make one of their specialities, a soup, which represents the seven days of Creation, with Shabbat being the seventh day.

Every year, the new season's produce is eagerly anticipated, and as each vegetable is tasted for the first time, it is customary to recite the Shehehayanu, a prayer of thanksgiving.

THE ASHKENAZI TRADITION
Years of struggle and poverty, when Eastern European Jews were hounded from place to place, and taxed to the limit, made them increasingly inventive as to how they prepared vegetables. Carrots, cabbages, beetroot (beets), onions and turnips may have been dull and heavy but the Jews favoured their strong flavours. They frequently pickled vegetables to improve their taste, and to preserve them through the long winters. Sauerkraut, pickled cucumbers and borscht all date from this era.

When Ashkenazi Jews from Poland and Russia migrated south, they discovered a wealth of new vegetables. Peppers soon became

popular, partly because they pickled well, and could be dried to make paprika. Potatoes were eaten with great gusto because they were so tasty and filling, and aubergines (eggplants), which had made their way to Romania from Spain and Italy, became widely used. Tomatoes were not widely accepted for some time, as their red colour was the same hue as blood and there was some question as to whether or not they were kosher – which may account for the Ashkenazi speciality, pickled green tomatoes.

SALAD VEGETABLES
In the early days, raw vegetables and salads were not greatly appreciated by Ashkenazim raised in cold climates, where warming, filling stews were a necessity. However, radishes of several kinds were still enjoyed, along with raw turnips, cucumbers, raw onions and garlic. The young spring shoots of garlic were much prized, and were often eaten with dense black bread. Sometimes raw carrots were grated and eaten in salads, as were the young leaves of wild greens and herbs, although these were often cooked and eaten hot as well.

THE SEPHARDI TRADITION
The Jews of the Iberian Peninsula had a much greater variety of fresh vegetables available to them than their northern neighbours. They were among the first Europeans to encounter corn, (bell) peppers, tomatoes and green beans, which were introduced from the New

World, and they embraced them with enthusiasm. Jewish merchants helped to popularize these new vegetables by introducing them to the more remote parts of Spain and then, after their expulsion in 1492, to the wider world. Globe artichokes and pumpkins were reputedly brought to Italy by the Jews. So too were aubergines (eggplants), which were much valued for their meaty texture, particularly when meat itself was not available, or had to be omitted because of the presence of dairy foods.

Sephardi Jews have always been known for their love of vegetables. They add them to stews, pilaffs and soups. Because they cook with olive oil, vegetable dishes are *pareve* so may be served with meat or dairy. They are cooked simply, then dressed with olive oil and lemon juice.

Vegetables also make perfect partners for eggs. Sephardi specialities range from the North African turmeric-tinted potato omelette, a variation on tortilla, to the Sicilian spinach tortino and a Spanish-Syrian dish of aubergine with eggs and cheese. The repertoire also includes chakshouka, a delicious Arabian dish consisting of (bell) peppers, tomatoes and eggs.

ABOVE: *Colourful warm weather vegetables such as (bell) peppers, globe artichokes and aubergines (eggplants) form the basis of many Sephardi dishes.*

From the deli counter

Potato salad, coleslaw, cucumber and onions, Russian salad, roasted peppers, Romanian aubergine (eggplant) salad and marinated mixed vegetables are just some of the vegetable offerings that can be found in the deli. Sauerkraut is another deli staple, while dill pickles are the star attraction. American deli kosher dill pickles are not made with added sweetening or vinegar, just brine with spices and lots of garlic. More recently, specialities from Israel such as baba ghanoush have become popular.

RIGHT: *Tubs of coleslaw, dill pickles and potato salad are just a few of the delectable offerings found in the deli.*

Fruit, nuts and seeds

Fruit has always been important to the Jewish table. The first fruits of every season are the subject of specific blessings, with special affection being reserved for melons, figs, dates and grapes, because of their prominent place in the Bible. Nuts and seeds are also widely eaten, providing protein and variety to many dishes.

FRUITS

All fresh fruits are considered kosher and, for some very strict Jews, it is the only food they will eat if they are not sure of the Kashrut of a kitchen. Fresh fruit can be eaten whole, uncut by *treyf* (not kosher) knives.

Israel is one of the world's leading fruit growers. Jaffa oranges, juicy grapefruit, kumquats and tiny lime- and lemonquats are grown for local consumption and export, alongside persimmons (Sharon fruit) from the Sharon valley and delicious avocados.

TRADITIONS

At Sukkot a lulav (citron) is used for making the blessings over the Sukkah. At Rosh Hashanah, apples are dipped in honey, pomegranates are eaten to celebrate fertility and abundance, quinces are baked and preserved and challah often contains dried fruit.

Ashkenazim make charoset, the fruit and nut paste enjoyed at Pesach, from apples and walnuts, while Sephardim favour tropical fruits and dried fruits. At Tu b'Shevat, Jews taste their way through a variety of orchard fruit, and at Chanukkah, apple sauce is served with potato latkes.

REGIONAL SPECIALITIES

Sephardim, living in lush, warm climates, have always enjoyed a wide variety of fruits including figs, dates, melons and citrus fruits. Quinces are traditionally made into sweet preserves for Rosh Hashanah, stuffed for Sukkot, candied for Pesach, and added to meat stews at other times. Another speciality of the Sephardi Jews, particularly those from North Africa, are preserved lemons that have been pickled in brine. They are also often added to savoury dishes such as spicy meat stews.

Fruit was not as easily available to the Ashkenazim and soft and deciduous fruits were a seasonal delight for them. Raspberries, gooseberries, currants, cherries, plums, pears and apples were enjoyed in many dishes from pancakes and pastries to fruit soups, cakes and compotes. Baked apples filled with brown sugar and cinnamon are one of the classics of the Ashkenazi kitchen.

Surplus harvest was often dried or preserved and enjoyed during the rest of the year when the fruits were out of season. Compotes made of dried fruit are still very popular in the Ashkenazi kitchen.

LEFT: *Apples, plums and cherries are fruits of the Ashkenazi table.*

LEFT: *Quinces, dates and figs are among the warm weather fruits of the Sephardi table.*

Dried fruit is also often used in cakes and strudels as well as added to many meat dishes. Raisins are frequently added to meatballs and pie fillings, and the classic tzimmes (a savoury meat or vegetable stew) is enriched with the addition of dried apricots and prunes.

Making fruit soup

Classic Ashkenazi fruit soup makes a refreshing start or end to a meal. Plums, cherries or red berries give a good result, but any fruit can be used.

1 Chop 1.3kg/3lb fruit and place in a large non-reactive pan. Add 1 litre/ 1³/₄ pints/4 cups water, 475ml/ 16fl oz/2 cups dry white or red wine and the juice of 1 lemon. Stir in a little sugar, honey and cinnamon. Bring to the boil, then leave to simmer until the fruit is tender.

2 Mix 10ml/2 tsp arrowroot with 15ml/1 tbsp cold water. Stir into the soup, then bring to the boil and cook, stirring, until thickened.

3 Remove from the heat, stir in a little more water or wine if the soup seems too thick, then stir in a dash of vanilla extract. If using peaches, cherries or apricots, add almond extract instead. Allow to cool, then chill. Serve with sour cream or yogurt.

NUTS AND SEEDS

These are pareve and enjoyed by both Ashkenazim and Sephardim. They may be added to sweet or savoury dishes as an ingredient or eaten on

their own as a snack. Street stalls in Israeli cities sell toasted nuts and seeds, known as garinim, for nibbling.

Almonds are used in sweet and savoury dishes. Mandelbrot (hard almond cookies) are among the classic sweets of the Ashkenazi kitchen, whereas almond paste is a favourite filling used in the filo pastries of North Africa and Mediterranean countries.

Pistachio nuts are enjoyed throughout the Middle East. Toasted and salted, they are a favourite snack. Unsalted pistachio nuts are crushed and layered into sweet desserts such as baklava, cake fillings and cookies. Poppy seeds are particularly popular with the Ashkenazim. They are eaten in cakes such as the classic Russian mohn torte and sprinkled on top of breads such as bagels. Their flavour is intensified when they are roasted and ground to a paste, to be used as a filling for cakes and pastries.

Sesame seeds can be purchased whole or hulled, raw or toasted. For optimum flavour, buy raw hulled seeds. Just before use, toast them in a heavy, ungreased pan until fragrant and golden. Toasted sesame seeds can be crushed to make halva or tahini, or simmered with honey or sugar to make sumsum, crisp confections that are sold as street food in Israel. Walnuts are widely used in Ashkenazi cooking and are an essential ingredient in charosset,

a paste of nuts, spices, wine and fruit representing the mortar the Jews used to build the pyramids, traditionally eaten at Pesach.

ABOVE: *Almonds, sesame seeds and poppy seeds are widely used in traditional Jewish cooking.*

Treats from the deli

The sweet aroma of baked apples welcomes visitors to the deli. Fruit compotes and jellies, and rice puddings studded with dried fruit are all available. Apricot leather – a paste of cooked apricots, dried in sheets or strips, and eaten as a confection or warmed with boiling water until it reverts to a thick paste – is also a deli speciality. Dates are coated with coconut or stuffed with nuts and sold in blocks. Delis with a large Middle Eastern clientele have jars of sweet preserves, ready to be spooned out and eaten with plain cake. Green walnuts, cherries, plums and kumquats are all stewed in honey and sold in this way.

Herbs and flavourings

The Ashkenazim used the flavourings of Eastern Europe to create their robust and often piquant dishes, while the Sephardim used their own local flavourings to create a cuisine that is richly spiced and aromatic.

HERBS AND SPICES

A special place is reserved for herbs and spices in the rituals of the Jewish table. Both mild and bitter herbs are eaten at Pesach, while the sweet aroma of cinnamon, ginger, nutmeg and cloves is inhaled as part of the havdalah ceremony that signifies the end of Shabbat, the smell of the spices welcoming the week ahead.

Ashkenazim adopted the flavours of Eastern European cooking: young dill fronds, parsley, spring onions (scallions) and tender young garlic. Spices were also added to cakes and breads and occasionally meat dishes. A mixture of herbs and spices was used in pickled vegetables, meats and fish, contributing to their piquant flavours.

Countries with a strong German and Russian heritage introduced Jewish settlers to mustards of various kinds. In delis today you will find a large selection of mustards, such as wholegrain, smooth, sweet and herbed, ready to add their flavour to all manner of Ashkenazi dishes.

In Hungary, Ashkenazi Jews encountered paprika, and soon embraced it, making their own versions of dishes dominated by this warm, yet subtle, spice, such as chicken paprikash and the classic meat goulash.

In the same eclectic fashion, Jewish people embraced other flavours typical of all the different lands in which they lived: thyme and oregano from the Mediterranean region; cumin and coriander from India; cinnamon and harissa from North Africa and chillies from Mexico.

On the wondrous palette of Middle Eastern cooking, spice mixtures are the culinary colours. They add fragrance and flavour to whatever they touch. Middle Eastern

ABOVE: *Cumin and coriander seeds are favoured in the North African kitchen, while paprika is essential in Hungarian Jewish cooking.*

spice blends are many and varied and may be dry ground mixtures or wet pastes made with fresh chillies, garlic and herbs. Spice blends taste much more intense if they are made from freshly roasted and ground spices.

Making harissa

This hot, spicy paste is used extensively in Tunisian and other North African cooking. It is based on medium-sized chillies with a medium hot flavour. The blend is widely sold in jars, but it is easy to make your own.

1 Put 10–15 whole dried chillies in a pan with enough water to cover. Bring to the boil, then remove from the heat.

2 When the chillies are cool enough to handle, carefully remove the stems, seeds and membrane, then pound to a purée with 10 garlic cloves, and 5ml/1 tsp each of ground coriander, caraway and cumin in a mortar with a pestle.

3 Add 2.5ml/^{1}/$_2$ tsp salt and 15ml/ 1 tbsp extra virgin olive oil to the mixture. Stir in enough cold water to make a thick paste.

Making hawaij

This fragrant mixture of spices comes from Yemen. It is delicious in stews, soups and sauces.

1 Place 30ml/2 tbsp black peppercorns and 15ml/1 tbsp caraway seeds in a spice grinder, or use a pestle and mortar.

2 Add 10ml/2 tsp each of ground cumin and turmeric, 5ml/1 tsp cardamom seeds and several pinches of saffron threads. Process to a powder and keep in a tightly sealed jar in a cool, dark place.

Making berbere

This Ethiopian spice mixture is based on hot chillies.

1 Mix 90g/3¹/2oz paprika with 10ml/2 tsp cayenne pepper, the seeds from 20 cardamom pods, 2.5ml/¹/2 tsp ground fenugreek seeds, 1.5ml/¹/4 tsp each of ground ginger and freshly grated nutmeg, and generous pinches of black pepper, cloves, ground cinnamon and allspice.

2 Lightly toast the mixture in a hot, ungreased pan for less than a minute. When cool, store in a sealed jar.

Making chermoula

This moist mixture of herbs, spices and aromatics comes from North Africa. It is mainly used as a marinade for fish but is also good with chicken, potatoes and other vegetables.

1 In a bowl, combine 75ml/5 tbsp extra virgin olive oil with 30ml/2 tbsp lemon juice, 4–5 crushed garlic cloves and 10ml/2 tsp ground cumin.

2 Stir 15ml/1 tbsp paprika, 1.5ml/¹/4 tsp ground ginger and 1 chopped fresh chilli or a pinch of chilli powder into the spice mixture.

3 Add 90ml/6 tbsp chopped fresh coriander (cilantro) leaves and a little flat leaf parsley or mint, if you like, to the bowl, season with salt and mix well or purée to a smooth paste.

FLAVOURINGS

There are a number of other flavouring ingredients that play an essential role in Jewish cooking. Salt is not just used as a seasoning but also plays a role in ritual, especially in kashering. It is seen as a purifying agent and, in biblical times, it was sacrificed at the Temple in Jerusalem. In Morocco, Jews sprinkle salt on newborn babies, to ward off the evil eye. At the Pesach Seder, it is dissolved in water and used to represent the tears of Israelite slaves. Sour salt (citric acid) is a great favourite in the Ashkenazi kitchen and is used instead of lemon to add a sour taste to dishes such as borscht. Honey has been much loved by Jews since the biblical description of Israel as a land flowing with milk and honey. It is used to represent the sweetness of the year to come at Rosh Hashanah.

Rose water and orange flower water are fragrant essences used in sweet and savoury dishes. They are added to the syrups poured over sweet pastries, and couscous dishes. Halek, also known as dibis, is a thick date syrup used to flavour foods. It is available in jars, but you can make your own. Reconstitute dried dates in water, then boil in a little water until soft. Purée, then strain into a pan and cook over a medium heat until thick.

Karpas and moror

These are the herbs that feature at Pesach. Karpas is the mild herb eaten at the Seder meal. It might be leaves of young lettuce, as favoured in the Sephardi tradition, or parsley, as favoured by the Ashkenazim. Moror are the bitter herbs, eaten as a reminder of the tears shed by Hebrew slaves in Egypt. Grated horseradish is often used, or the bitter greens might be represented by chicory (Belgian endive) or watercress.

Noodles, pancakes, dumplings and savoury pastries

Noodles were once the pride of the Ashkenazi kitchen, and were cut into a variety of shapes, then served in soup, tossed with sour cream or cheese, or layered with other ingredients and baked into puddings known as kugels. Since biblical times pancakes have been very popular. They are usually either very thin and filled or thick and crispy. Generations of Jewish cooks have delighted in dumplings, especially knaidlach made from matzo meal and egg. Savoury pastries are popular with both Ashkenazi and Sephardi Jews.

NOODLES

These were probably introduced to German Ashkenazi kitchens during the 14th century, via the Italian Jews. This was long before they reached the non-Jewish German kitchen during the 16th century. Pasta came to Poland at the same time, possibly through Central Asia, and the Yiddish word for noodles (*lokshen*) comes from the Polish word *lokszyn*. The sauces of the Polish Yiddish kitchen also showed a Central Asian slant. They were based on yogurt, sour cream and fresh cheeses, rather than the rich tomato

RIGHT: *Lokshen, farfel, varnishkes and plaetschen are just a few of the classic noodles from the Ashkenazi kitchen.*

sauces of Italian extraction. Sephardi cooking showed a more distinctive Italian or Spanish influence, as evidenced in kelsonnes, dumplings filled with cheese and eaten at the festival of Shavuot, and calzonicchi, which are filled with spinach and enjoyed for Purim.

Making noodle dough

Egg noodles are still made at home for special occasions. This is easy to do with a pasta-rolling machine, but they can also be rolled by hand on a well-floured surface.

1 Sift 225g/8oz/2 cups plain (all-purpose) flour and 2.5ml/½ tsp salt into a large bowl, making a well in the centre.

2 Pour two lightly beaten eggs into the flour and mix with a fork, gradually incorporating the eggs into the flour. Continue to stir, using a wooden spoon, until combined. Alternatively, place all the ingredients in a food processor fitted with the metal blade and mix to form a dough.

3 Turn the dough on to a floured board and knead until smooth and elastic. Place in a plastic bag, seal and leave for at least 30 minutes.

4 If using a pasta-rolling machine, roll out walnut-size balls of the dough, then, one at a time, feed the dough into the largest opening of the rollers. Fold the flattened dough and repeat, reducing the roller opening until the dough is the desired thickness.

5 If rolling by hand, divide the dough into three equal pieces, then roll out each piece on a floured surface, until it is extremely thin.

Making noodle shapes

Lightly sprinkle the sheets of rolled noodle dough with flour, then cut into the desired shape. To cook, drop the pasta into a large pan of boiling salted water and cook for 2–4 minutes.

To make lokshen (flat noodles), roll a sheet of noodle dough into a tight scroll. Using a sharp knife, cut the dough crossways into narrow or wide strips, as desired. Unroll the strips, boil and serve with sauce, in soup or baked together with other ingredients in a kugel.

To make plaetschen (little squares), cut a sheet of noodle dough into 1cm/½in squares. Boil and then serve in soup.

To make varnishkes (butterflies), cut a sheet of noodle dough into 2.5cm/1in squares. Pinch each square in the centre to form a bow tie or butterfly. Boil and serve in soup or with kasha.

To make farfel (pellets), grate kneaded, unrolled noodle dough through the large holes of a grater to form pellets. Boil and add to soups.

PANCAKES

In times of plenty, pancakes were made from the best ingredients; when times were hard they were made from whatever wild greens could be found.

Crêpe-like blintzes are filled with cheese, meat, fruit or vegetables and often folded into parcels and fried until crisp. Thick, hearty latkes are a treat often eaten at Chanukkah, consisting of grated potatoes formed into cakes and fried.

Chremslach are thick pancakes eaten at Pesach. They are made from egg, matzo meal and seasonings and served with sour cream or yogurt.

Ataif are Egyptian pancakes, raised with yeast and served with a sweet syrup and clotted cream.

DUMPLINGS

The word knaidlach comes from *knodel*, the German for dumpling. Knaidlach are as much a part of Yiddish cooking as dumplings are of Eastern European peasant food. Because they were made with matzo, knaidlach were eaten for Shabbat and other festivals, especially Pesach, when bread is forbidden.

Sephardi dumplings are made from noodles stuffed with meat, then floated in soup. Alternatively, they may be made from rice.

SAVOURY PASTRIES

Whenever there was something special to celebrate, the women of both Ashkenazi and Sephardi communities would gather and spend many days preparing different kinds of pastries.

Classic Ashkenazi pastries include knishes (half-moon shaped turnovers), strudels (wafer-thin pastry rolled around fillings) and piroshkis (small pies). They may be filled with kasha,

mashed potatoes and onions, minced (ground) meat, browned cabbage, chopped egg and sometimes smoked salmon. They are baked or fried.

The Sephardim have a virtually endless number of savoury pastries, made with many different types of pastry – from delicate fried filo pastry to crisp, crumbly shortcrust – and filling. They are made in an array of shapes, including half moons, squares, triangles, rectangles, circles and even cones and round balls, and they may be baked or deep-fried in oil.

Breads

The world over, bread is very important to the Jews. A meal without bread is not a meal, according to the dictates of the Jewish religion. Without bread, there can be no hamotzi (blessing over the bread that signals the start of a meal) and neither can there be the Birkat Hamazon (grace, which usually concludes a meal). A meal without bread can only really be considered a snack.

ABOVE: *Challah is the traditional bread of Shabbat and festivals and may be braided, round or shaped like a ladder, depending on the festival.*

ASHKENAZI BREADS

In Jewish bakeries, it is usual for the breads to be *pareve* – made without butter or milk so that they can be eaten with either meat or dairy foods. There is challah, rye bread, pumpernickel, bagels, Kaiser rolls and onion rolls – the variety is astonishing and, if you happen to have wandered into an ethnic Jewish bakery, you may well encounter some wonderful regional specialities as well as the usual fare.

All ethnic groups have a wide variety of breads, both for everyday use and special occasions. When the Ukrainian Ashkenazim emigrated to America, they brought with them sourdough loaves of seeded rye, dark pumpernickel and onion-crusted rolls. Walking into one of their bakeries is a joy: the smells of baking – yeast, flour, a whiff of something sweet – mingling with the scent of the wood-burning stove.

Bagels are an Ashkenazi classic that travelled from the shtetlach and ghettos of Eastern Europe and are now enjoyed all over the world. They lend themselves to any number of different fillings and are very satisfyingly chewy.

Bagels are usually made in bakeries that bake nothing else, because the procedure for making them is a special one. The dough rings are first briefly

ABOVE: *Pumpernickel, from the Ashkenazi tradition, is dark and sour with a crisp crust.*

poached in huge vats of water before being glazed and baked. This technique creates the distinctive dense, chewy texture that has made bagels so popular. To walk past a bagel bakery without venturing in is just about impossible. The alluring smell inevitably entices you in, and you'll want to get yourself a nice hot bagel before setting off once more.

Sweet challah is the traditional Shabbat and festival bread of the Ashkenazi Jews. The dough is made with eggs and vegetable oil, which gives it a soft texture, similar to that of brioche, and is lightly sweetened with honey or sugar.

The loaves are usually braided, made with three, six or even twelve strands of dough. During Rosh Hashanah challah may be shaped into a round or crown, in honour of the Rosh Hashanah blessing: "The whole world will crown thee." On the eve of Yom Kippur, the challah is shaped like a ladder, raised arms or wings, representing prayers rising heavenwards.

Boulkas are small, individual challah rolls, shaped into rounds, braids or spirals and dusted with poppy seeds, that are frequently served at weddings.

SEPHARDI BREADS

These vary greatly and are very different from the breads of the Ashkenazim. Some are risen; some are flat; some, such as melawah, are slightly puffed and fried to a crisp. One Sephardi bread most of us are familiar with is pitta, a flat bread favoured by Jews and Arabs alike, and by many other Middle Easterners as well. Iraqi pitta bread is a large flat bread, which resembles an enormous, thick pancake.

Breads that are especially made for the Sabbath include mouna, lahuhua and kubaneh. A coiled bread from Yemen, kubaneh is made from a rich yeast dough. It is prepared

RIGHT: Jews eat unleavened matzos at Pesach but they are also enjoyed during the rest of the year.

before the Sabbath begins, then steamed in a very low oven overnight.

Israel produces a marvellous array of breads, from the simple everyday loaf, which is crusty on the outside and beautifully tender inside, to large flat breads, which are used for wrapping around vegetables or meat.

MATZOS

These are unleavened breads, made especially for Pesach, when leavened bread may not be eaten. The flat, brittle matzo sheets are served at the table, and are also ground to make a meal that is transformed into cakes, biscuits and cookies. Matzo meal can be either fine or coarse, while matzo farfel is lightly crushed matzo.

For Pesach, matzos are prepared under special guidelines and the packaging must always be marked "Kosher for Pesach". Observant Jews often eat schmurah matzo, which is always handmade to an extremely high specification.

LEFT: Pitta bread came from the Middle East but is now enjoyed by Ashkenazim, Europeans and Americans alike.

From the deli counter

Oy what sandwiches! A true Jewish deli sandwich is a thing of mammoth proportions. Piles of salami, billows of roasted turkey, peppery pastrami, corned or salt beef, bologna or steamed knockwurst are just some of the possible ingredients, and most likely there will be a combination of several of them, at least 350g/12oz per sandwich, layered between thick slices of fresh, crusty, tender bread. A sandwich from one of the legendary New York delis, such as the Carnegie or Second Avenue Deli, Katz's, the Stage Deli or Juniors will be far too thick for the average eater.

ABOVE: A bagel filled with cream cheese and wafer-thin slices of smoked salmon is the quintessential Jewish deli snack.

Cakes and pastries

For Jews, whenever there is something to celebrate, be it a festival or a family occasion, cakes and other sweet treats are very much in evidence. Precisely what is on the table will largely depend on whether the hosts come from the Ashkenazi or Sephardi traditions, as these take very different approaches when it comes to baking.

During Pesach, the kosher kitchens of both Ashkenazim and Sephardim undergo a transformation. At this time, all food must be free of leaven, and eggs are used as the main raising agent instead. The result is a wealth of featherlight sponge cakes, often made with matzo meal and ground nuts.

BELOW (LEFT TO RIGHT): *Traditional Ashkenazi rugelach and mandelbrot cookies are delicious with a glass of hot tea.*

THE ASHKENAZI BAKERY
Visit an Eastern European bakery and you will find the shelves filled with a wide selection of delectable pastries, sweetmeats, crisp cookies, cakes and crunchy rolls. No one could possibly walk through without having a "little something". A cup of coffee is never just a cup of coffee: you must have a Danish – a pastry filled with jam and topped with icing (frosting) – or a rugelach, or maybe a mohn cake or strudel, or perhaps an apfelkuchen. The choice and variety is endless.

Cakes of all kinds are baked in the Ashkenazi kitchen. Kuchen is closer to a sweet fruit bread than a cake. It is made from a sweet dough, filled with fresh or dried fruit. Honey cake, also known as lekach, is eaten for Rosh Hashanah and Shabbat, while almond cakes, plava and other leaven-free cakes are classic Pesach specialities. For Purim, the traditional treat is hamantashen, triangular cakes filled with seeds and fruit.

Cookies and sweet biscuits include croissant-shaped rugelach, almond mandelbrot and plain kichel. None of these are very sweet, and they make the perfect accompaniment to tea. Teiglach, from Lithuania, are rich with honey, so a little goes a long way.

ABOVE: *Sweet, fruit-filled strudel made with paper-thin pastry is one of the glories of the Eastern European Jews.*

Candied orange peel, known as pomerantzen, is a great favourite of all Jews, not just because it tastes so good, but because the peel that might otherwise have been discarded is transformed into an irresistible treat.

Jews love pastries, the most well known being strudel, which originated as a hefty pastry roll filled with vegetables or fruit. It was the Turks, invading Hungary in 1526, who introduced the very thin multi-layered pastry that we now know as strudel dough.

Strudel is eaten for many festivals: with cabbage for Simchat Torah; with dried fruit for Tu b'Shevat; with crushed poppy-seed paste for Purim and with cheese for Shavuot. Fruit versions are filled with sliced apple, cherries or rhubarb, alone or with dried fruit.

Making strudel pastry

This is very like filo pastry, which can be bought ready-made and makes a good substitute for strudel pastry.

1 In a bowl, beat 250g/9oz/generous 1 cup butter with 30ml/2 tbsp sugar and 250ml/8fl oz/1 cup sour cream or softened vanilla ice cream. Add 2.5ml/$\frac{1}{2}$ tsp vanilla extract and 1.5ml/$\frac{1}{4}$ tsp salt, then stir in 500g/1$\frac{1}{4}$lb/5 cups plain (all-purpose) flour. Mix to a soft dough.

2 Divide the dough into three pieces, wrap separately and chill overnight (or freeze for up to 3 months).

3 If necessary, thaw the dough. Place one piece on a floured board. Flatten it lightly, then, very gently, pull it out with your hands, pulling each side in turn until it is almost paper thin. It is now ready to fill and bake.

SEPHARDI SWEET SPECIALITIES

These are Mediterranean in their origin. Every Sephardi community produces a wealth of moist, succulent almond and walnut cakes. Often a local dish was adapted for Jewish holidays – Greek Jews eat crisp, fried loukomades for Chanukkah, Israelis eat jam-filled sufganiot (doughnuts) and Tunisians enjoy syrup-soaked cakes for Purim.

During Pesach, when leaven may not be used, many cookies and cakes are made with nuts. Almond cakes, coconut macaroons and sesame seed halva are favourites.

Syrup-soaked filo pastries, such as baklava, are popular among Sephardi Jews. Other pastries include kaddaif, a shredded pastry drenched in syrup, and felabis, deep-fried, pretzel-like pastries filled with syrup.

Making simple baklava

The secret to perfect baklava is to pour very cold syrup over a hot pastry, or very hot syrup over a cold pastry.

1 Preheat the oven to 200°C/400°F/Gas 6. Layer six sheets of filo pastry in a shallow ovenproof dish, brushing each layer with melted butter or oil.

2 Sprinkle chopped nuts on top of the pastry, to a depth of 1cm/$\frac{1}{2}$in.

3 Sprinkle generously with sugar and cinnamon. Top with six more layers of buttered or oiled filo, then cut the top layer of pastry into triangles.

4 Bake for 30 minutes until golden. Remove from the oven and pour over hattar, or a light syrup flavoured with orange flower water or rose water.

The deli cheesecake

This is one of the most popular desserts in the deli cabinet. It is often associated with Ashkenazim from Germany, who were famous for their fresh cheeses. It is eaten at Shavuot, reflecting the legend of the Jews who, on returning to camp after receiving the Torah, found that their milk had turned sour and had to sweeten it with honey.

Cheesecakes can be flavoured and topped with many ingredients from fruit to chocolate and it is not unusual to find delis offering upwards of 30 different types.

BELOW: *Cheesecake is a deli classic, though purists argue that only a simple white cheesecake can be considered the real thing.*

Glossary

BAGELS
Bread rolls with a hole in the middle, symbolizing the circle of life. They are boiled before being baked.

BAKLAVA
A crisp pastry of filo and nuts soaked in a honey syrup, which is often flavoured with rose or orange flower water or sweet spices.

BAR/BAT MITZVAH
The coming of age ceremony for a boy (bar) or girl (bat) in which they assume the religious duties and responsibilities of an adult. A boy reaches this age at 13 years old, a girl at 12 years old.

BESAN
See gram flour.

BETZA/BEITZAH/BAITZAH
Hebrew for egg. Betza are eaten by all Jewish communities and are considered *pareve*; they play an important role in the ritual plate for the Pesach Seder.

BLINTZ
A thin pancake rolled around a savoury or sweet filling. They are often fried.

BORSCHT
Soup of Ashkenazi origins made from beetroot (beet) and sometimes other vegetables; eaten hot or cold.

BOTARGA
Sephardi salted or smoked dried fish roe such as sea bass and grey mullet.

BRIK
A deep-fried Moroccan-Tunisian pastry made from warka dough. Tuna and egg is a very popular filling.

CHANUKKAH
The festival of lights commemorating the Maccabean victory over the Seleucians in 165BCE (BC). Also known as Hanukkah.

CHAROSSES/CHAROSSET
The paste of nuts, spices, wine and fruit eaten at Pesach to symbolize the mortar used by the Jews to build the pyramids. Also known as Harosset.

CHASSIDIM
A movement of Observant Jews originating in Poland, the Ukraine and Galicia.

CHELLOU
Persian rice, cooked with butter and allowed to form a crisp bottom crust. Vegetables, herbs, fruits and nuts may be added.

CHERMOULA
A Moroccan spice and herb paste, often used with fish.

CHICKPEA FLOUR
See gram flour.

CHOLENT
Ashkenazi, long-simmered stew of meat and beans.

CHRAIN
Horseradish and beetroot condiment of Ashkenazi origin.

CHREMSLACH
Ashkenazi matzo meal pancakes, often eaten at Pesach.

DAFINA
A long-baked Shabbat stew, made of beef (often with a cow's foot), potato, beans and hard-boiled eggs. It is a speciality of Moroccan Jews.

DAIRY
Refers to a meal made with milk products.

DESAYUNO
Sephardi Shabbat breakfast.

EINBREN FLOUR
Flour browned with fat. Traditionally, it is used to thicken soup in the German Ashkenazi kitchen.

EINGEMACHTS
A preserve made from beetroot (beets), radishes, carrots, cherries, lemons or walnuts. It is favoured at Pesach.

ETROG
Large yellow citron used to celebrate Sukkot.

FALAFEL
Deep-fried chickpea or broad (fava) bean croquettes, adopted from the Arabs. They are eaten with salads and pitta bread.

FARFEL
Pellet-shaped dumplings made from grated noodle dough or crumbled matzo.

FASSOULIA
White beans, often stewed with meats and vegetables, eaten as an appetizer or stew, popular with the Jews of Greece.

GEFILTE FISH
Ashkenazi balls of minced (ground) fish, eaten cold, poached and jellied or fried. Gefilte means stuffed, and originally the fish was stuffed back into its skin.

GLATT
A particularly stringent form of Kashrut.

GRAM FLOUR
It is made from ground dried chickpeas and is used in pakoras, spicy pastries, and falafel.

HALEK
Date syrup, eaten for Pesach by the Jews of Iraq, India and Yemen, in addition to or in place of charosses. In the Bible, "halek" is thought to refer to honey.

HALVA
A sweetmeat made from sesame paste and sugar or honey, and flavourings, then pressed into blocks and dried. Chocolate, pistachio nuts or almonds may also be added. Halva is popular with Jews from Middle Eastern and Balkan lands.

HAMANTASHEN
Triangular-shaped, Ashkenazi cookies with various fillings such as apricots or nuts; eaten at Purim.

HAMIM
See cholent.

HANUKKAH
See Chanukkah.

HARISSA
North African fiery paste of red chillies and spices, often served with mild foods such as couscous.

HAROSSET/HAROSSETH
See charosses/charosset.

HAVDALAH
The ceremony that marks the end of Shabbat and the start of the new week. Prayers are said over wine, special spices are smelled, and a candle is lit.

HAWAIJ
A Yemeni spice mixture that includes cardamom, saffron and turmeric, used in most Yemenite cooking.

HILBEH
A pungent spice paste of ground fenugreek seeds, often served with spicy zchug. Hilbeh is slighly bitter and has a unique aroma, almost like brown sugar.

HOLISHKES
Ashkenazi stuffed cabbage, it is often simmered or baked in a sweet-and-sour tomato sauce.

HOREF
Hebrew for hot pepper or spicy. Used in Israel to describe the spicy sauce or peppers eaten with falafel.

IKADDAIF
Shredded dough used in Middle Eastern pastries to wrap around nuts, then baked and soaked in syrup.

KAES
The Yiddish word for cheese.

KAMA
A Moroccan spice mixture of pepper, turmeric, ginger, cumin and nutmeg, used for stews and soups.

KARPAS
The parsley, lettuce or herbs placed on the Seder plate and dipped in salt water.

KASHA
Toasted buckwheat.

KASHRUT
Jewish dietary laws dictating what may be eaten.

KATCHAPURI
Flaky pastries filled with goat's cheese or feta cheese, brought to Israel from Georgian Russia.

KHORESHT
The sweet and sour Persian stew that is ladled over rice and features in the everyday diet of Persian Jews.

KIBBEH
Dumplings of Middle Eastern origin made from minced (ground) lamb and soaked bulgur wheat, eaten either raw, formed into patties and baked or fried, or layered with vegetables and baked.

KICHELACH
Light, crisp, slightly sweet cookies of Lithuanian Ashkenazi origin. They are traditional in areas where there is a large Ashkenazi population.

KIDDUSH
Sanctifying blessing over the wine and challah.

KINDLI
Another name for Ashkenazi poppy-seed cake.

KISHKE
Stuffed intestine filled with matzo, chicken fat, onion and paprika. It is served roasted or poached.

KLOPS
Meatloaf or meatballs of Ashkenazi German origin.

KNAIDLACH/KNAIDL
Matzo meal dumplings.

KNISH
Savoury pastry filled with meat, cheese, potato or kasha.

KOSHER
Term used to describe any food deemed fit to eat by the laws of Kashrut.

KOSHER SALT
Large grains of salt for sprinkling on to meat, to drain out blood, as stipulated in the laws of Kashrut.

KREPLACH
Small meat-filled dumplings made of noodle dough, often served in chicken soup. At Shavuot they are filled with cheese and eaten with fruit and sour cream.

KRUPNIK
Ashkenazi mushroom and barley soup. It is a traditional dish in Eastern Europe, particularly Poland, Lithuania and Ukraine.

KUBBEH
Meat dumplings favoured by Iraqi Jews as well as those who emigrated to India and Israel. Kubbeh are eaten in soups and stews, and may also be steamed or fried.

KUBANEH
A Sephardi Shabbat breakfast dish cooked for a long time, often overnight.

KUCHEN
An Ashkenazi yeast-raised cake that is slightly sweet and often stuffed with fruit. It is eaten with coffee or tea for morning or afternoon breaks, or as dessert for festivals or holiday meals.

KUGEL
Baked dish of noodles, vegetables, potatoes or bread; it may be sweet or savoury.

LAG B'OMER
Holiday falling on the 33rd day of the counting of the Omer, the days between Pesach and Shavuot.

LAHUHUA
A Yemenite flat bread that has a crumpet-like texture and is eaten with soups and stews.

LATKES
Fried potato pancakes eaten by Ashkenazi Jews at Chanukkah. Latkes can also be made with other vegetables or matzo meal.

LEKAKH
Traditional honey cake.

LOKSHEN
Yiddish for noodles.

LOX
Yiddish for smoked salmon.

LUBIA
Black-eyed beans (peas), popular in Sephardi cooking, especially in Israel where they are added to spicy soups and stews.

MAMALIGA
A creamy porridge-like mixture of cornmeal, similar to polenta. It can be eaten hot or cold.

MANDELBROT
Almond cookies resembling Italian biscotti. They are double-baked, giving a crisp, hard texture.

MANDLEN
The Yiddish word for almonds, which are favoured in Ashkenazi cooking. Also the name of the crisp, baked or fried soup garnishes made from noodle dough.

MAROR
Bitter herbs eaten at Pesach.

MATJESHERRING
See salt herring.

MATZO/MATZAH
The unleavened, thin brittle bread ritually eaten during Pesach.

MATZO
A fine flour made from crushed matzo, used to make cakes, popular among Turks.

PAREVE
Yiddish, describing the neutral foods that are neither dairy nor meat.

PASTRAMI
A cured dried beef that is a speciality of the USA.

PESACH/PASSOVER
The festival that celebrates the Israelites' exodus from Egypt.

PETCHA
Calf's foot jelly, a traditional Ashkenazi dish.

PIEROGI
Little pasta dumplings, of Polish origin, filled with fillings such as cabbage, mashed potatoes, onions, cheese and kasha and served with sour cream. The sweet, dessert version are varenikes.

PIROSHKI
Ashkenazi savoury pastries of Russian origin made with a yeast dough and filled with cabbage, meat, hard-boiled egg, spinach, cheese or kasha. They may be appetizers or large pastries, and baked or fried.

PITTA BREAD
Known as khubz in Arabic, pitta is a round flat bread that is cooked on a flat pan and puffs up as it cooks. The bread may be slashed open and its hollow inside filled like a sandwich.

PLAETSCHEN
Ashkenazi term for little squares of pasta, which are eaten in soup.

PLAVA
Very simple Ashkenazi sponge cake. It was once the favourite British Jewish cake and every bakery in London's East End had its own version.

POMERANTZEN
Candied citrus peel, a classic sweet treat of the Ashkenazi Jews of Eastern Europe, especially Germany. Sometimes it may be dipped in chocolate.

PORGE
Ritually remove blood and fat from meat.

POTATO FLOUR
Used as a light and translucent thickening agent for sauces and cakes.

PRESERVED LEMONS
A North African speciality, lemons are salted and layered in jars, which imparts a tangy flavour. They are often added to dishes such as tagines and salads.

PURIM
Festival celebrating the rescue of the Jewish people from Haman, as described in the Book of Esther.

RAS AL HANOUT
A Moroccan spice mixture that literally means head of the shop. Ras al hanout can contain myriad ingredients, and each spice shop guards its own secret recipe.

ROSH HASHANAH
The Jewish New Year, literally meaning head of the year.

RUGELACH
Crisp, Ashkenazi cinnamon-and-sugar layered biscuits (cookies).

RYE BREAD
A typical bread from Eastern Europe, especially the Ukraine, where it is made with sourdough studded with caraway seeds. It is often baked on a cornmeal-coated baking sheet and is, therefore, sometimes known as corn rye.

SALT HERRING
Herring preserved in wooden barrels in layers of salt.

SAUERKRAUT
Fermented, pickled cabbage, made by salting shredded cabbage. It is a staple of the people of Eastern and parts of Western Europe.

SCHAV
A refreshing, sour green soup made from sorrel and eaten cold. It is a traditional Ashkenazi soup and can be bought in bottles in American delis.

SCHMALTZ
Yiddish for fat, usually referring to rendered chicken fat.

SCHMALTZ HERRING
See salt herring.

SCHNITZEL
Tender escalopes (US scallops) of meat or poultry, coated in crumbs and fried. They originate from Vienna.

SEDER
The ceremonial dinner eaten on the eve of Pesach, commemorating the flight of the Jews from Egypt.

SEPHARDIM
Jews who settled in Iberia (Spain and Portugal), after the destruction of the Second Temple, when they were banished from Jerusalem.

SHABBAT
Religious day of rest, which is a Saturday.

SHALACH MANOT
Food given at Purim.

SHALET
Baked Ashkenazi dessert of apple and eggs, favoured by the Jews of Alsace. Other ingredients such as matzo, challah, dried fruit and spices may be added.

SHAVUOT
Feast of the weeks, commemorating the revelation of the Ten Commandments.

SHOCHET
The ritual butcher, licensed to slaughter and prepare meat according the laws of Kashrut.

SHTETL
Yiddish for the Jewish villages of Eastern Europe.

SHULCHAN ARUKH
A code of Jewish law.

SIMCHAT TORAH
The festival of the Torah, celebrated by parading the Torah through the synagogue.

SOUR SALT
Citric acid, a souring agent used in Russia and in traditional Jewish cooking. It is available in crystals or grains.

SPAETZEL
Tiny dumplings made of noodle dough, dripped into boiling water. Also known as farfel.

STRUDEL
Eastern European speciality of crisp, layered pastry filled with fruit, sprinkled with sugar and served as a mid-afternoon treat with tea. Strudel can also be savoury, filled with vegetables, meat and sometimes fish.

SUFGANIOT
Israeli jam-filled doughnuts, eaten to celebrate Chanukkah.

SUKKOT
The autumn harvest festival, the celebration of which includes eating meals in gaily decorated three-walled huts known as sukkah.

SUMAC/SUMAK
A sour-tasting, red spice made from ground berries of the sumac plant. Israelis, and some Sephardim, sprinkle the spice over salads, breads and rice.

TAHINA/TAHINI
A Middle Eastern paste of toasted hulled sesame seeds, mixed with lemon juice, garlic and spices, and thinned with water. It is eaten as a sauce, dip, or ingredient in dishes such as hummus.

TEIGLACH
Ashkenazi cookies that have been cooked in honey. They are a Lithuanian speciality, which are popular in communities that celebrate their Lithuanian origins, such as South Africa. They are favoured at Rosh Hashanah when sweet foods are eaten in hope of a sweet new year.

TORAH
The scroll used in the synagogue, consisting of the first five books of the Bible, which include the Ten Commandments. The Torah was given to the Jews by God on Mount Sinai.

TORSHI
Pickled vegetables, eaten throughout the Middle East, especially Persia.

TREYF
Meaning not kosher. Also known as tref and trefah.

TU B'SHEVAT
Festival known as the birthday of the trees.

TZIMMES
A sweet dish of carrots, vegetables, dried fruit and sweetening agent such as honey or sugar. Spices, and sometimes meat, are added.

VARENIKES
Ashkenazi fruit-filled pasta dumplings filled with dried apricots, cherries or prunes.

VARNISHKES
Noodles shaped like bow ties or butterflies, often served with kasha.

WARKA
Very thin, transparent pastry from Morocco.

WAT/WOT
Spicy Ethiopian stew, enjoyed by the Bene Israel (Ethiopian Jews). It is often eaten for Shabbat.

YOM KIPPUR
The Day of Atonement, a solemn holy day upon which fasting is strictly observed.

ZAHTAR/ZA'ATAR
This is both the name of the wild herbs that grow in the hillsides of Israel and the Middle East, and the name of the spice mixture made with them, which includes zahtar, ground cumin, toasted sesame seeds, coriander seeds and sometimes a little sumac and/or crushed toasted hazelnuts. Zahtar is eaten for breakfast, as a dip with fresh pitta bread, a drizzle of olive oil and fresh goat's cheese.

ZCHUG/ZHUG/ZHOUG
This Yemenite seasoning paste is one of Israel's most popular spice mixtures. It may be red, based on chillies, garlic, spices, coriander (cilantro) and parsley, or green, with more herbs and less or no tomatoes.

ZEROA
A lamb's bone, often a shank, roasted and placed on the ritual plate for Pesach. It represents the sacrificial lambs eaten on the eve of the flight of the Jews from Eygpt.

Index